BE HOLY

BE HOLY

A
Catholic's
Guide
to
the
Spiritual
Life

FATHER THOMAS G. MORROW
Foreword by Archbishop Donald W. Wuerl

Note: The editors of this volume have made minor changes in capitalization to some of the Scripture quotations herein. Please consult the original source for proper capitalization.

The stories herein are true, but some incidentals have been changed to protect the privacy of those involved.

Cover and book design by Mark Sullivan
Cover image © istockphoto.com/Nic Taylor

LIBRARY OF CONGRESS CATALOGING-IN-PUBLICATION DATA
Morrow, T. G.
Be holy : a Catholic's guide to the spiritual life / T.G. Morrow.
p. cm.
Includes bibliographical references and index.
ISBN 978-0-86716-878-5 (pbk. : alk. paper) 1. Holiness—Catholic Church. 2. Spiritual life—Catholic Church. 3. Christian life—Catholic authors. I. Title.
BX2350.3.M665 2009
248.4'82—dc22

2009020727

ISBN 978-0-86716-878-5

Published by Servant Books, an imprint of St. Anthony Messenger Press.
28 W. Liberty St.
Cincinnati, OH 45202
www.ServantBooks.org

Printed in the United States of America.

Printed on acid-free paper.

09 10 11 12 13 5 4 3 2 1

. . . . .

This work is dedicated to Mary,
who brought Jesus to us
and brings us to Jesus.

. . . . .

. . . . .

CONTENTS

. . . . .

FOREWORD

In the procession following Mass, as I leave the Great Upper Church of the Basilica of the National Shrine of the Immaculate Conception in Washington, D.C., I am reminded of the vocation of each of us, the universal call to holiness. Stretching across the back wall of the basilica is a finely sculpted stone frieze that can be seen from anywhere in the nave or sanctuary. In it ordinary people, men and women from many walks of life, are drawn forward and ultimately together as they focus on the Holy Spirit, depicted by a dove.

The movement of this work of art is interesting in that it leads its viewer to keep moving forward, out of the doors of the Upper Church, into the world. The life of holiness is one that is meant for each individual and is lived in the midst of family, work, recreation and all the activity in which we find ourselves.

Our contemporary culture has a great interest in spirituality. Corporations offer "executive retreats" and bookstores have shelves devoted to spirituality. A hunger for the spiritual life exists deeply in the soul of the human person, and yet for many Catholics, the rich tradition of Catholic spirituality that addresses the hunger remains an untold secret. Amid all of the books, manuals and programs we can find under the topic of "spirituality," it is sometimes difficult to know what is authentically Christian and genuinely Catholic.

Be Holy: A Catholic's Guide to the Spiritual Life addresses those who want to live holy lives but need some practical starting points. Father Thomas Morrow sensibly reminds us to look first at what he describes as the "tried and true" of Catholic tradition when looking for ways to enrich our spiritual life. He draws from Scripture, the writings of a rich variety of the doctors of the Church, other saints and spiritual writers to outline how one can grow in holiness. He illustrates how prayer, participation in the sacraments, and the practice of the spiritual and corporal works of mercy form the foundation for holy living.

The saints can serve as our practical guide to holiness. Their lives were in some ways very ordinary and busy, and yet they kept a focus on Christ, which directed them to love God well. Just as some of our greatest saints learned to make time for Eucharistic Adoration, Father Morrow suggests that, in addition to a commitment to prayer and frequent reception of the sacraments, contemporary men and women with their increasingly busy lives can also make time for adoration and thus receive the graces of this devotion. Furthermore, as Christ himself and many saints have taught us, love of our Lord is expressed in love of our neighbor. In the third part of the book, Father Morrow explores how we can love our neighbor through the practice of the spiritual and corporal works of mercy.

My hope is that *Be Holy: A Catholic's Guide to the Spiritual Life* will help readers grow in appreciation of the many gifts Christ has given to assist us as we make our way toward union with God in heaven. As Father Morrow reminds us, "holiness is the happiest way to live" because it brings us to share forever in the life of the Holy Trinity.

. . . . .

Most Reverend Donald W. Wuerl, S.T.D.
Archbishop of Washington

INTRODUCTION

A young boy told his mother once, "I don't want to go to heaven."

"Why not?" she asked.

"Because I think it's boring," he responded.

The mother realized she had a major task: to prove to her son that heaven is certainly not boring and in fact is the most exciting, delightful place we could ever imagine. She must have done a good job. Her son now goes all over the country to tell his conversion story to Catholic youth.

Alas, many people nowadays think that heaven is boring, hell is empty and purgatory is like a doctor's waiting room. Not so, according to Christ and his Church. Far from it!

There is no way we can overestimate the tremendous happiness of heaven, nor the horror of hell and the great suffering of purgatory for those who do not take seriously the universal call to holiness (*Lumen Gentium*, 40). It seems certain that if more people kept in mind that they will surely die one day and meet the Lord—at which time their eternal destiny will be sealed—they might be more dedicated to preparing for that crucial day. This is a powerful motivation to live the gospel.

How do we get to heaven? Some suggest that being a "good guy," not being mean or nasty to others, is enough. Others propose that helping others will do it. Still others claim that we just need to avoid sin.

We should be deeply aware of the grace-empowered effort it will take to get to heaven. Yet the way is straightforward: Pursue the life of grace, and seek to become a new creation in Christ by living the virtues. Through prayer, the sacraments, the Mass and reading the lives of the saints, we can begin on the path to holiness and stay motivated. Through striving for virtue and cultivating the fruits of the Holy Spirit, we can become the saints God intended us to be.

It does not matter what success we have in this world, if we are rich or famous or have scores of wonderful friends, if we don't make it to the kingdom, all is wasted. Our blessed Lord said as much: "For what will it profit a man, if he gains the whole world and forfeits his life? Or what shall a man give in return for his life?" (Matthew 16:26)

If you were to die tomorrow and had to admit to the Lord, "I confess, I hadn't come to love You with all my heart, soul and mind," He would, we might speculate, be very understanding. But if you died tomorrow and had to admit that you not only had not come to this level of love but had no *plan* as to how to get there, you should anticipate some great displeasure on His part. We *need* a plan. And that is the subject of this book.

. . . . .

PART ONE

Motivations

for

Holiness

CHAPTER ONE

The Delight of Heaven: The Divine Marriage

Saint Augustine was born of a womanizing father but a devout mother, and in his early years he took after his father. He moved in with his mistress at the age of sixteen and lived with her for the next fourteen years. Meanwhile his mother, Monica, prayed for him without ceasing.

At the age of thirty-one Augustine had a conversion, and he began to pray and do penance for his past life of sin in preparation for baptism. Eighteen months after his baptism, his mother died, happy to see the answer to her prayers, and three years later Augustine was ordained a priest. Four years after that he became a bishop. He became one of the most prolific writers the Church has ever known.

Augustine wrote beautifully of his conversion, especially in this passage from his autobiography:

> Too late have I loved you, O Beauty so ancient and so new.... I...rushed headlong after these things of beauty which you have made.... They kept me far from you, those fair things which, were they not in you, would not exist at all.... You have sent forth fragrance, and I have drawn in my breath, and I pant after you. I have tasted you, and I hunger and thirst after you. You have touched me and I have burned for your peace.[1]

Augustine had tasted the illicit delights of this world and was perceptive enough to realize that they didn't satisfy. After just a taste of heaven, experienced through prayer and fasting, he realized that all beauty, all joys of this world are just a whisper of the beauty and joy to be found in God, in this life and in the life to come.

The first task of every Christian, of every person, is to discover the unfathomable glory of being united with God, now and forever. But first we must find motivation in the goal God has given us, namely heaven.

Heavenly Basics

Our Blessed Lord refers to heaven, using several different terms, about 170 times in the Gospels. He uses the terms *heaven, kingdom of heaven, kingdom of God, life* and *eternal life* to describe the place of eternal reward. He often speaks of the kingdom of heaven by comparing it to things we are familiar with on earth:

> The kingdom of heaven is like a treasure hidden in a field, which a man found and covered up; then in his joy he goes and sells all that he has and buys that field.
>
> Again, the kingdom of heaven is like a merchant in search of fine pearls, who, on finding one pearl of great value, went and sold all that he had and bought it. (Matthew 13:44–46)

Twice the Lord speaks of the kingdom as being like a wedding feast (see Matthew 22:1–14; 25:1–13), as does the author of the book of Revelation (Revelation 19:7–8). Thus our Lord clearly speaks of the kingdom of heaven as something very valuable, worth selling all you have to possess, as a feast celebrating a commitment of love and as a rich reward for whatever sacrifice we make here on earth.

Saint Paul speaks of heaven in glowing terms: "What no eye has seen, nor ear heard, / nor the heart of man conceived, / what God has prepared for those who love him" (1 Corinthians 2:9).

Will everyone be at the same level in heaven, or will some receive a greater reward than others? We find the answer in Church teaching: "[The souls of those who enter heaven] clearly behold the triune God as he is, yet one person more perfectly than another according to the difference of their merits."[2] This is based on the words of our Lord, "The Son of man...will reward each one according to his conduct" (Matthew 16:27, author's translation), and the words of Saint Paul, "[E]ach shall receive his wages according to his labor" (1 Corinthians 3:8; see also 2 Corinthians 9:6).

Many of the saints wrote of the tremendous joy that awaits those who are worthy of heaven. To paraphrase Saint Augustine, what must be the amazing joy of those in heaven, seeing how much beauty, how many delights and what great blessings we enjoy on earth? Teresa of Ávila remarked, "Our life lasts only for a couple of hours; our reward is boundless."[3]

"Were [the soul] to have but a foreglimpse of the height and beauty of God," Saint John of the Cross wrote, "she would not only desire death in order to see Him now forever, as she here desires, but she would very gladly undergo a thousand singularly bitter deaths to see Him only for a moment; / and having seen Him, she would ask to suffer just as many more that she might see Him for another moment."[4]

What is heaven like? Do we have any clues that it is more than just a place with many clouds and gold streets?

Heaven is primarily a relationship. But what sort of a relationship?

The Divine Marriage
Saint Gregory the Great said heaven would be like a marriage: "The husband of every Christian soul is God; for she is joined to

Him by faith."[5] Saint John of the Cross wrote along the same lines:

> One does not reach this garden of full transformation which is the joy, delight, and glory of spiritual marriage, without first passing through the spiritual espousal and the loyal and mutual love of betrothed persons. For, after the soul has been for some time the betrothed of the Son of God in gentle and complete love, God calls her and places her in His flowering garden to consummate this most joyful state of marriage with Him.... Yet in this life this union cannot be perfect, although it is beyond words and thought.[6]

Thus, according to John, the "spiritual marriage" begins here. Saint Teresa of Ávila's experience confirms this. In 1572 the Lord said to her, "[Y]ou will be My bride from today on. Until now you have not merited this; from now on not only will you look after My honor as [that of] your Creator, King, and God, but...as My true bride."[7] Others, including Saints Margaret of Cortona, Catherine of Siena, Lawrence Justinian, John of God and John Vianney, received wedding rings from the Lord.[8]

When Saint Margaret Mary Alacoque suffered great temptations against her vocation to be a nun, Jesus appeared to her one day after Communion and showed her that He was "the most beautiful, the wealthiest, the most powerful, the most perfect and the most accomplished [among] all lovers."[9] He told her He had chosen her to be His spouse. After this she hesitated no more!

There are several biblical passages that support this marriage-with-God theme. In Ezekiel 16 the Lord addresses His people, Jerusalem, as His unfaithful spouse with whom He later will restore His covenant. In Isaiah 62 we read:

No more shall men call you "Forsaken,"
  or your land "Desolate,"
But you shall be called "My Delight,"
  and your land "Espoused."
For the LORD delights in you,
  and makes your land his spouse.
As a young man marries a virgin
  your Builder shall marry you;
And as a bridegroom rejoices in his bride
  so shall your God rejoice in you.
(Isaiah 62:4, 5, *NAB*)

The book of Hosea contains God's complaint against Israel: "[T]he land commits great harlotry by forsaking the LORD" (Hosea 1:2). God leads Israel back to Him and says after her return, "I will espouse you for ever; I will espouse you in righteousness and in justice, in steadfast love, and in mercy. I will espouse you in faithfulness; and you shall know the LORD" (Hosea 2:19–20).

The Call to Holiness

The implications of this heavenly marriage are important. A marriage in which one party loves at an intensely high level and the other loves feebly simply won't do. If we are to be in a marriage with God, who is so holy, we must be holy ourselves. We must somehow be energized or supercharged to love God at least at a quasi-reciprocal level. We must love God with *His* power—in other words, with *His* Spirit.

How much of the Holy Spirit do we need to be in this marriage? It doesn't take a rocket scientist to know it takes 100 percent: that is, we must be filled to capacity. The more the Holy Spirit dwells within us, the more we are ready for this marriage.

If you had the spirit of Mozart, you could write great music. If you had the spirit of Shakespeare, you could write great plays. But if you have the Spirit of God, you can love at a quasi-divine level.

This need for profound holiness is fully supported elsewhere in Sacred Scripture. In Luke 10:27 we are told that the condition for entering eternal life is to "love the Lord your God with all your heart, and with all your soul, and with all your strength, and with all your mind; and your neighbor as yourself." Jesus said in Matthew 5:48, "You, therefore, must be perfect, as your heavenly Father is perfect." In Leviticus 19:2 we read, "Be holy, for I, the LORD your God, am holy" (NAB, see also Leviticus 11:45; 20:7). In addition we read in Ephesians 1:4, "[H]e chose us in him before the foundation of the world, that we should be holy and blameless before him" (also see Ephesians 5:27; 1 Peter 1:15, 16; 2:5).

Vatican II speaks of this call to holiness: "Thus it is evident to everyone, that all the faithful of Christ of whatever rank or status, are called to the fullness of the Christian life and to the perfection of charity; by this holiness as such a more human manner of living is promoted in this earthly society" (Lumen Gentium, 40).

The Lord appeared to Saint Margaret Mary at one point and told her, "Learn that I am a Holy Master and One that teaches holiness, I am pure and cannot endure the slightest stain."[10] Thus it should be clear: To live in this heavenly marriage with God we must be *very* holy.

How foolish we would be to underestimate the holiness at which we must arrive in order to be worthy of the kingdom. Living in the state of grace is enough to be saved, that is, to be worthy of purgatory. And as we shall see in chapter three, purgatory is not a pleasant prospect. To be worthy of entering the kingdom, we must surrender all.

Loving God at the quasi-divine level is no easy task. Nor is loving our neighbor as ourselves. Jesus told us it would be hard: "Enter by the narrow gate; for the gate is wide and the way is easy, that leads to [eternal] destruction, and those who enter by it are many. For the gate is narrow and the way is hard, that leads to [eternal] life, and those who find it are few" (Matthew 7:13–14). Elsewhere he said, "[Whoever] would come after me, let him deny himself and take up his cross and follow me" (Mark 8:34). Clearly the path to this level of love is a difficult one.

However, Jesus promised that he would sweeten the journey: "Come to me, all who labor and are heavy laden, and I will give you rest. Take my yoke upon you, and learn from me; for I am gentle and lowly in heart, and you will find rest for your souls. For my yoke is easy [or gentle], and my burden is light" (Matthew 11:28–30).

Imagine Heaven

Saint John of the Cross wrote of the beauty of the encounter with God:

> Since the virtues of the bride are perfect and she enjoys habitual peace in the visits of her Beloved, she sometimes has a sublime enjoyment of their sweetness and fragrance when her Beloved touches these virtues, just as a man enjoys the sweetness and beauty of flowers and lilies when they have blossomed, and he must handle them....
>
> ...The soul feels that the Beloved is within her as in His own bed. She offers herself together with her virtues, which is the greatest service she can render Him. Thus one of the most remarkable delights she receives in her interior communion with God comes from this gift of herself to her Beloved.[11]

We should think often of the utter delight of heaven. Imagine being married to the most desirable member of the opposite sex you could ever conceive of.[12] A chaste embrace with the God who created in His own image the beauties we so desire on earth, and who has called us to be His spouse, is an image that is a mere whisper of the delight and the glory of heaven. And by using this sort of healthy fantasy, we can inspire ourselves to strive harder in prayer and other spiritual activities.

We might pray thus:

O God, I have always dreamed of a lover like You: beautiful to the core beyond telling, kind, charming, alluring, fascinating, unfathomable and faithful. You are so warmly inviting, yet you graciously and firmly correct my selfishness. Oh, that you might always call me to that intimate eucharistic union with you, body and soul, even in my imperfect but sincere love, as a sign and promise of the ecstatic intimacy to which you call me in the eternal marriage of Your kingdom, an intimacy that married couples on earth could never dream of.

No doubt for some this romantic approach to God might seem strange or even uncomfortable. Yet it is fully in accord with the Scriptures and the writings of the saints. Hosea 1 and 2 and Ezekiel 16 are examples of how the prophets, as Pope Benedict XVI wrote, "described God's passion for His people using boldly erotic images."[13] The Song of Songs and Saint John of the Cross's *Spiritual Canticle* are further expressions of this recurring theme of God as our passionate, intimate Lover.

Ultimately it is only union with this Beloved that will fulfill us completely as persons, and an imaginary embrace of such a Lover is noble fantasy, a powerful sign of that intimate union.

And it is more real than any earthly fantasy could ever be. Such an image should move us to pray and worship our God, that we might be worthy of this eternal, joyful, peaceful divine marriage, with this "beauty so ancient and so new."

We should contemplate this joyful reality called heaven several times—even scores of times—daily, that we might be ever aware of our purpose on this earth: to become worthy to live in that kingdom of love forever.

. . . . .

CHAPTER TWO

The Reality of Hell

In this age of pseudo-sophistication, the mention of hell is considered much too harsh for polite company. But the saints did not shy from mentioning it. On the contrary, Saint Josemaría Escrivá wrote, "There is a hell. A trite enough statement, you think. I will repeat it, then: there is a hell! Echo it, at the right moment in the ears of one friend, and another, and another."[1]

I heard of one Catholic who said in public, "If there is a hell, there's no one there." Alas, there is no evidence to support such a statement in Scripture, in the teaching of the Church or in the writings of the saints.

Our Lord refers to hell and its punishment fewer than thirty times in the Gospels, compared to about 170 references to heaven. Thus his emphasis is certainly on the positive, but he does not leave out the negative. He uses the terms *Hades* and *Gehenna*, both translated as "hell," but more often speaks of fire, everlasting fire or unquenchable fire.

> [I]f your foot causes you to sin, cut it off; it is better for you to enter life lame than with two feet to be thrown into hell. And if your eye causes you to sin, pluck it out; it is better for you to enter the kingdom of God with one eye than with two eyes to be thrown into hell, where their worm does not die, and the fire is not quenched. (Mark 9:45–48)

Of course, here our Lord is not literally suggesting that anyone should cut off his hand or tear out his eye. He uses these comparisons simply to indicate the terrible nature of hell and the sin that sends one there. It seems He accomplished His goal very well, for the words are truly frightening.

A concept that arose in the twelfth century speaks of two pains in hell: the pain of loss, of not seeing God; and the pain of sense, a burning sensation. Saint Catherine of Siena received this insight from the Lord: "[The souls in hell] see themselves deprived of the vision of Me, which is such pain to them, that, were it possible, they would rather choose the fire, and the tortures and torments, and to see Me, than to be without the torments and not to see Me."[2] Thus the pain of not seeing God is far more agonizing than the pain of sense.

Freedom and Love

Many people through the ages have had difficulty imagining that there is such a thing as hell, in light of all the revelations about God's goodness and mercy. The doctrine of hell is truly a mystery with which we must struggle, even after it has clearly been spelled out to us. And yet the Church doctors were all agreed on their acceptance of this doctrine. Saint Augustine wrote, "[Hell] is not a matter of feeling, but a fact.... [T]here is no way of waiving or weakening the words which the Lord has told us He will pronounce at the Last Judgment."[3]

The mystery of hell is wrapped up with our freedom and the justice of God. Although God is all-merciful, one who enters hell has rejected God's mercy, and God does not overrule his choice. Consider the following simple analogy.

Let's say you come upon someone trying to solve a problem on his computer that you solved on your own computer the previous year. And suppose you offer him some advice, explaining that you had the same problem a year ago and it took you six months to solve it. "If you want," you explain, "I can help you get it fixed in about half an hour."

But let's say he rejects your offer, saying, "Look, I don't need your help. I can fix it myself."

You can't very well force him to accept your help. Thus he is left to his problem, which he may *never* solve. You might say as you leave, "If you change your mind, call me."

So it is with the Lord. He comes along and tells us He has the answer to *all* our problems: Live according to His way. But if we reject His offer, He cannot, without denying our freedom (and thus the merit of our love), force us to accept Him. Thus He must leave us in our self-chosen misery of having rejected God, who is infinitely good. In a sense He says, "If you change your mind, call Me."

This is how a person can choose hell. In order to be free to love, we must be free to refuse to love. If God were to force us to love, we'd all be robots.

There is, of course, no way of knowing who *does* go to hell, but our blessed Lord warned us, "Enter by the narrow gate; for the gate is wide and the way is easy, that leads to [eternal] destruction, and those who enter by it are many. For the gate is narrow and the way is hard, that leads to [eternal] life, and those who find it are few" (Matthew 7:13, 14). He also said, "[M]any are called, but few are chosen" (Matthew 22:14).

Some people wonder if perhaps, at some point in time, hell might end and all the souls might be released. This is not a new idea. Origen, a theologian in the early Church, believed, as did some others, that hell would not last for all eternity. However, the Church condemned this idea at its Fourth Lateran Council.

This was no doubt based on the use of the word *eternal* or *everlasting* in Scripture when describing the punishment of hell (see Matthew 25:41, 46; 2 Thessalonians 1:9).

Wisdom From the Saints

The saints were not shy about speaking of hell. Saint Francis de Sales dedicated a chapter in his *Introduction to the Devout Life* to a reflection on hell. He wrote:

> Picture to yourself a dark city, reeking with the flames of sulphur and brimstone, inhabited by citizens who cannot get forth.
>
> ...
>
> Even so the lost are plunged in their infernal abyss;—suffering indescribable torture in every sense and every member; and that because having used their members and senses for sin, it is just that through them they should suffer now. Those eyes which delighted in impure vicious sights, now behold devils; the ears which took pleasure in unholy words, now are deafened with yells of despair;.... Beyond all these sufferings, there is one greater still, the privation and pain of loss of God's Glory, which is for ever denied to their vision....
>
> Consider how insupportable the pains of Hell will be by reason of their eternal duration. If the irritating bite of an insect, or the restlessness of fever, makes an ordinary night seem so long and tedious, how terrible will the endless night of eternity be, where nothing will be found save despair, blasphemy and fury![4]

Saint Ignatius of Loyola included a similar meditation on hell in his *Spiritual Exercises*.[5]

Saint Bernard of Clairvaux urged us to go down into hell now (by way of imagination) so that we don't end up there when we die. Saint John Chrysostom said something similar: "What can be more grievous than hell? Yet nothing is more profitable than the fear of it."[6]

Saint Teresa of Ávila relates the following:

[W]hile I was in prayer one day, I suddenly found that, without knowing how, I had seemingly been put in hell. I understood that the Lord wanted me to see the place the devils had prepared there for me and which I merited because of my sins....

...I experienced a fire in the soul that I don't know how I could describe. The bodily pains were so unbearable that though I had suffered excruciating ones in this life, and according to what the doctors say, the worst that can be suffered on earth (for all my nerves were shrunken when I was paralyzed...), these were all nothing in comparison with the ones I experienced there. I saw furthermore that they would go on without end.... This, however, was nothing next to the soul's agonizing: a constriction, a suffocation, an affliction so keenly deeply felt...that I don't know how to word it strongly enough.[7]

Hell is real. As Saint Augustine said, we can't get around the fact that there is a hell, and Jesus said people go there. Our primary focus should be on heaven, but when we become lazy about our spiritual life, we should heed the words of Saint Bernard, Saint Ignatius and Saint Francis de Sales: Think about going to hell. That should wake us up!

. . . . .

CHAPTER THREE

The Suffering of Purgatory

We might ask, what if you begin to grow in holiness, and you come to the point where you are in the state of grace and love God with *most* of your heart, soul and mind but not all. And you love your neighbor *nearly* as much as you love yourself. And you die. Where would you go?

Not to heaven, since Jesus said you must love God with *all* your heart, soul and mind and your neighbor as yourself to have everlasting life. You wouldn't go to hell, since you died in the state of grace. You would go to purgatory.

The dogma of purgatory is an all-but-forgotten teaching of the Church, yet it is extremely valuable in supporting the call to perfection. The fundamental purpose of purgatory is not forgiveness of sins but *making up* for sins, reparation. The damage done by sin, especially to our own souls, is "repaired" in purgatory.

When a boy accidentally throws a baseball through a neighbor's window, it is one thing to be forgiven by the owner, another thing to repair the window. When a man does something terrible to his wife, it is one thing to receive her forgiveness, quite another to make it up to her. True, Jesus has paid the price for sin, but we have a relatively small price to pay as well. Saint Paul says, "Now I rejoice in my sufferings for your sake and in my flesh I complete what is lacking in Christ's afflictions, for the sake of his body, that is, the Church" (Colossians 1:24).

Paul thus indicates that we have a part to play in making reparation for sin.

The biblical support for purgatory is found, among other passages, in Saint Paul:

> Each one's work will become manifest; for the Day will disclose it, because it will be revealed with fire, and the fire will test what sort of work each one has done. If the work which any man has built on the foundation survives, he will receive a reward. If anyone's work is burned up, he will suffer loss, though he himself will be saved, but only as through fire. (1 Corinthians 3:13–15)[1]

Purgatory is a painful proposition. It was defined as a dogma of the Church at the Council of Trent in 1563.[2] The *Catechism of the Catholic Church* teaches:

> The Church gives the name Purgatory to this final purification of the elect, which is entirely different from the punishment of the damned. The Church formulated her doctrine of faith on Purgatory especially at the Councils of Florence and Trent. The tradition of the Church, by reference to certain texts of Scripture, speaks of a cleansing fire: "As for certain lesser faults, we must believe that, before the Final Judgment, there is a purifying fire." (*CCC*, #1031 quoting Gregory the Great, *Dial.* 4, 39: PL77, 396; cf. *Mt* 12:3)

Joyful Pain

Saint Catherine of Genoa wrote: "[T]he divine essence is so pure and light-filled / —much more than we can imagine— / that the soul that has but the slightest imperfection / would rather throw itself into a thousand hells / than appear thus before the divine presence."[3] And the Anglican C.S. Lewis wrote: "Our souls demand purgatory, don't they? Would it not break the heart if

God said to us, 'It is true, my son, that your breath smells and your rags drip with mud and slime, but we are charitable here and no one will upbraid you with these things, nor draw away from you. Enter into the joy'? Should we not reply, 'With submission, sir, and if there is no objection, I'd rather be *cleaned* first.' 'It may hurt, you know.' 'Even so, sir.'"[4]

To deny the doctrine of purgatory would be to make hollow Christ's teaching that we must be made perfect as our heavenly Father and that we should love God with *all* our heart, soul and mind and love our neighbor *as* ourselves. Is it reasonable to think that if we fall far short of this perfection but die in the state of grace, Jesus will meet us at the gates of heaven and say, "That teaching on perfection—I didn't really mean it. Come on in"?

Saint Augustine wrote: "This fire of Purgatory will be more severe than any pain that can be felt, seen or conceived in this world."[5] Thomas Aquinas taught something similar: "In Purgatory there will be a twofold pain; one will be the pain of loss, namely the delay of the divine vision, and the pain of sense, namely punishment by corporeal fire. With regard to both the least pain of Purgatory surpasses the greatest pain of this life."[6]

Saint Francis de Sales balances this misery with a certain sweetness for the souls in purgatory: "Their bitterest anguish is soothed by a certain profound peace. It is a species of Hell as regards the suffering; it is a Paradise as regards the delight infused into their hearts by charity—Charity, stronger than death and more powerful than Hell."[7]

Why is there such joy in purgatory? Because once we are there, we are sure of entering heaven one day. It's guaranteed.

Nonetheless, despite the delight of those being cleansed, the Church calls them the "Church Suffering." Several souls from purgatory have appeared to various saints, and I know of none who has said, "It's delightful here. Come and join me!" All have rather asked for prayers, penances or Masses to expedite their release.

The Horror of Sin

Why is purgatory so terribly painful? Because sin is so terribly horrible. Sin is totally incompatible with God, and as Jesus showed us on the cross, making reparation for sin is a painful thing. Alas, we have lost the sense of sin and with it the sense of purgatory's harshness.

Saint Ignatius of Loyola proposed as a "second mode of humility" that we come to say, "[I would not], for the sake of all creation or for the purpose of saving my life, consider committing a single venial sin."[8] Saint Catherine of Genoa wrote:

When I beheld that vision in which I saw the magnitude of the stain of even one least sin against God, I know not why I did not die. I said: "I no longer marvel that hell is so horrible, since it was made for sin; for even hell (as I have seen it) I do not believe to be really proportionate to the dreadfulness of sin; on the contrary, it seems to me that even in hell God is very merciful, since I have beheld the terrible stain caused by but one venial sin."[9]

Pope John Paul II taught in August of 1999:

[W]e are invited to "cleanse ourselves from every defilement of body and spirit" [2 Corinthians 7:1; see 1 John 3:3], because the encounter with God requires absolute purity.

Every trace of attachment to evil must be eliminated, every imperfection of the soul corrected. Purification must be complete, and indeed this is precisely what is meant by the Church's teaching on *purgatory*.[10]

Every time we sin, mortally or venially, we add to the debt. Can we "pay the debt" here on earth? Indeed we can! Saint Teresa of Avila said, "Let us praise God and strive to do penance in this life. How sweet will be the death of those who have done penance for all their sins, and [need] not to go to purgatory!"[11]

Pope Paul VI taught, "It is a divinely revealed truth that sins bring punishments inflicted by God's sanctity and justice. These must be expiated either on this earth through the sorrows, miseries and calamities of this life and above all through death, or else in the life beyond through fire and torments or 'purifying' punishments."[12]

And how much better it is to pay the debt in this life! Saint Catherine of Genoa wrote, "He who purifies himself from his faults in the present life satisfies with a penny a debt of a thousand [silver pieces]."[13]

You might ask, "What happens to a person who goes to confession, does his penance and is killed on his way home? Where would he most likely go?" Not to heaven. Most likely to purgatory.

"But he completed his penance," you say? Yes, but some historical perspective is needed here.

In the fourth and fifth centuries, the penance for one of the three major sins of murder, adultery or fornication and denying the faith was truly severe. A person might have to spend ten or fifteen years in penance for one instance of these. The married penitent could never again have relations with the spouse, and the single penitent could never *get* married.

Needless to say, people guilty of these things were not coming in great numbers to confession. They would put off going as long as possible, usually until their death was imminent. The Church noted this and began to ease up on the penances. It seems it was deemed best to get people forgiven as soon as possible, to preserve them from losing their souls even if the penances had to be reduced considerably. The penances became more and more symbolic, not representing all that might be needed to make up for the sins confessed.

And so it is today. Thus, for most people, going to confession and doing the penance does not necessarily prepare them to enter the kingdom. Some who are particularly holy would go directly to heaven, but most would need some additional purification.

Purgatory's Duration

Saint Robert Bellarmine, doctor of the Church, wrote, "There is no doubt that the pains of Purgatory are not limited to ten or twenty years, and that they last in some cases entire centuries."[14] Father Reginald Garrigou-Lagrange, a noted twentieth-century theologian, commented, "Theological opinion, in general, favors long duration of purgatorial purification. Private revelations mention three or four centuries, or even more, especially for those who have had high office and great responsibility."[15]

And it seems that, to the souls in purgatory, the time can seem much longer than the equivalent time on earth. Blessed James Alberione, founder of the Society of Saint Paul and the Daughters of Saint Paul, wrote,

> Regarding the duration of the pains of the suffering souls, we can recall some things which make us think deeply and fear greatly.... [A]bsolute duration is one thing and relative duration is another. The first is the time which the soul really spends in purgatory; the second is the impression which the soul has of this time. In other words, the soul which suffers but briefly believes that it has been

suffering for a long time. Many revelations say that only an hour in purgatory seems longer than a century.[16]

Saint Catherine of Genoa wrote, "If we regarded our own proper good, it would seem better to us to suffer here for a little than to remain in torments forever; better to suffer for a thousand years every woe possible to this body in this world, than to remain one hour in purgatory."[17]

And Father Garrigou-Lagrange wrote, "[P]urgatory is not measured by solar time, but by eviternity and discontinuous time. Discontinuous time...is composed of successive spiritual instants, and each of these instants may correspond to ten, twenty, thirty, sixty hours of our solar time."[18]

Eviternity (or æviternity), according to Saint Thomas Aquinas, "differs from time, and from eternity, as the mean between them both."[19]

So this is the fate of those who fail to take seriously the need to strive for perfection, or who take it seriously and don't quite make it but die in the state of grace: a painful yet confident existence for however many months or years or even centuries. And the soul's impression of time in purgatory may be much longer than its equivalent here on earth.

The Saints' Experiences

Don Bernardino de Mendoza, the brother of the bishop of Avila, had given Saint Teresa a house near Valladolid. When Teresa received news of Don Bernardino's death, the Lord told her that this man had been in danger of losing his soul, but Mary had interceded for him in gratitude for his donating the house for Teresa's order. He was in purgatory, and he would remain there until the first Mass occurred in that new house.

Although Teresa made every effort to expedite the founding of the new convent, she had to wait several months. When she finally had the first Mass said in the convent, she saw Bernardino standing next to the priest as she received Communion. He appeared in glory and thanked her for his release from purgatory.[20]

In November 1856 John Bosco's beloved mother and long-time helper died. Four years later she appeared to him in a dream. He asked her, "Are you happy?" Her reply was, "Very happy." He then asked, "Did you go straight to heaven when you died?" "No," was her abrupt response. This saintly woman had to spend time in purgatory before she entered heaven. This should be a reminder to all of the true holiness we must attain, by God's grace, in order to enter heaven.[21]

Saint Margaret Mary wrote of a Benedictine monk who appeared to her in a "pitiable condition," in a fire of which she herself felt the heat. He told her that because he had directed her to receive Holy Communion, he was given the grace to approach her and ask her to offer her sufferings and actions for him for three months to ease his pain. He told her he was in purgatory because he was too concerned about others' opinions of him, too attached to other people and not as charitable to his fellow monks as he should have been.

Saint Margaret Mary received permission from her superior to do as the monk asked. She endured terrible suffering, feeling the heat from his presence for the whole three months. After this he appeared to her in glory, about to enter heaven, and promised to help her from there.[22]

Teresa of Ávila related two experiences.

Eighteen or twenty years ago another nun died in the house I was in. She had always been sick and been a very good servant of God, devoted to her choir duties and most virtuous. I thought certainly she would not enter purgatory, because the illnesses she had suffered were many, and that she would have a surplus of merits. Four hours after her death, while reciting the hours of the Office before her burial, I understood she departed from purgatory and went to heaven.[23]

Another friar of our order, a truly very good friar, was seriously ill; while I was at Mass I became recollected and saw that he was dead and that he ascended into heaven without entering purgatory. He had died at the hour I saw him, according to what I learned later. I was amazed he hadn't entered purgatory. I understood that since he had been a friar who had observed his vows well the Bulls of the order about not entering purgatory were beneficial to him.[24]

Teresa said that from her visions, she was not aware of any soul that had gone directly to heaven besides the friar she mentioned above, Saint Peter of Alcántara and one Dominican priest.[25]

In summary then, purgatory is a very difficult prospect. If we fail to take seriously Jesus' call to perfection, we can anticipate much suffering. God does not want us to go to purgatory. He urges us to give totally of ourselves, to become holy, to become totally loving. May we heed His call!

. . . . .

. . . . .

CHAPTER FOUR

The Pursuit of Happiness

Every intelligent human being pursues happiness. No one in his right mind is intentionally seeking to be miserable. The key to finding this happiness is, of course, to seek it in the right places.

Anyone who knows the Christian faith realizes that *eternal* happiness lies only with God and in fulfilling his two great commandments of love. However, some have wondered if perhaps we must live boring, miserable lives on this earth in order to fulfill those commandments and then be rewarded with happiness when we die. In fact, nothing could be further from the truth.

If we look closely at the lives of the saints, we see very happy people, people who were truly fulfilled. Saint Francis of Assisi comes to mind immediately as someone who had virtually nothing in this world but was always joyful. Saint John Bosco, Saint Teresa of Ávila, Saint Thérèse of Lisieux, Saint John of the Cross, Saint Dominic Savio—they all found the "pearl of great price," and they were all happy about it.

The Scriptures proclaim the happiness that results from loving God:

Happy are we, O Israel,

for we know what is pleasing to God. (Baruch 4:4)

Blessed is the man who walks not in the counsel of the wicked,

nor stands in the way of sinners,

nor sits in the seat of scoffers;

but his delight is in the law of the LORD,

and on his law he meditates day and night.
He is like a tree
planted by streams of water, that yields its fruit in its season,
    and its leaf does not wither.
In all that he does, he prospers. (Psalm 1:1–3)

Happy the people whose God is the LORD! (Psalm 144:15)

Happy is he whose help is the God of Jacob,
whose hope is in the LORD his God. (Psalm 146:5)

To be near God is my happiness. (Psalm 73:28)[1]

Finding Fulfillment

Those who reject God tend to seek happiness in worldly things, such as pleasure, honor, comfort and wealth. However, if we look closely at the lives of those who have these things, we often find emptiness if not downright unhappiness and misery. The human heart longs for a richness, a profundity, that these things lack. This is why many people who seem to have much of this world's goods fall into drug or alcohol abuse and depression.

It seems that there are two things that fulfill us as persons: the first is knowing that we have made the lives of other people better—not just more pleasant but truly better. We call this love. The second is drawing close to others, intimacy. Intimacy often follows love and is its proper crown. But even if intimacy sometimes doesn't follow, love is still rewarding.

Although love and intimacy bring us pleasure, it is not the pleasure that fulfills us but the love and intimacy themselves, since they nourish the human heart. As Aristotle taught, pleasure is good only if it accompanies a morally good act. And even then pleasure is a fleeting thing.

It is no accident that Christianity provides love and intimacy *par excellence*. Loving God and neighbor are absolutely necessary for entry into the kingdom. Jesus stated this very clearly, as I indicated earlier.

> [A] lawyer stood up to put him to the test, saying, "Teacher, what [must] I do to inherit eternal life?" He said to him, "What is written in the law? What do you read there?" And he answered, "You shall love the Lord your God with all your heart, and with all your soul, and with all your strength, and with all your mind; and your neighbor as yourself." And he said to him, "You have answered right; do this, and you will live." (Luke 10:25–27)

A Christian who loves is fulfilling his human nature. He is doing what brings happiness. Pope John Paul II put it well: "Man cannot live without love. He remains a being that is incomprehensible for himself, his life is senseless, if love is not revealed to him, if he does not encounter love, if he does not experience it and make it his own, if he does not participate intimately in it."[2]

Vatican II said something similar: "[T]he Lord Jesus, when He prayed to the Father, 'that all may be one...as we are one' (John 17:21–22), opened up vistas closed to human reason, for He implied a certain likeness between the union of the divine Persons, and the unity of God's sons in truth and charity. This likeness reveals that man, who is the only creature on earth which God willed for itself, cannot fully find himself except through a sincere gift of himself" (*Gaudium et Spes*, 24).

By fulfilling the two commandments of love, the human person finds intimacy. Anyone who prays a good deal, receives the sacraments, attends Mass regularly and strives to grow in virtue will find himself very close to God. He will have a personal relationship with the God who loves him tenderly and passionately. He will also receive the power to love others as God loves them—unconditionally—and this will almost always bring about intimacy with these persons, especially those who are virtuous. Intimacy with the virtuous is a true joy.

Thus no one should think that we will have happiness only in heaven. It begins here. In fact, not only does heaven begin on earth for those who live the gospel, but hell begins here as well for those who don't.

Let us strive for heavenly happiness. The journey is hard but sweet.

The Meaning of Love

But how do we love God? And how do we love our neighbor? What exactly is meant by this word *love*?

The Greek word used in the Gospels is *agape*. Pope Benedect XVI wrote:

> By contrast with an indeterminate, "searching" love, this word [*agape*] expresses the experience of a love which involves a real discovery of the other, moving beyond the selfish character that prevailed earlier. Love now becomes concern and care for the other. No longer is it self-seeking, a sinking in the intoxication of happiness; instead it seeks the good of the beloved: it becomes renunciation and it is ready, and even willing, for sacrifice.[3]

We might define this love as a "giving of self for the good of the beloved without conditions or an unconditional active benevolence for the beloved." Certainly this is how God loves us.

Notice, it's not just an indiscriminate giving but a giving only if it is good for the one who receives it. I met a woman once who gave her son everything. Even in his mid-twenties she provided him with a place to stay without cost. She lent him money, which he never paid back. She gave him everything he asked for, and he became less and less able to do for himself. To make matters worse, the more she gave him the more he resented her (a common phenomenon).

It was only when the mother told her son to move out that he finally found a job and began to stand on his own two feet. Her excessive giving to her son, who was quite capable of supporting himself, had held him back and made him dependent on her.

Not all giving is love. In fact, some giving is done merely for self-gratification. In order to be love, the giving must always be for the good of the recipient. This is why God often refuses us what we ask for. Saint James put it well: "You ask and do not receive, because you ask wrongly, to spend it on your passions" (James 4:3).

And as we said earlier, this love is unconditional. The active concern for the good of the other is not tied to behavior or looks or good health. The Christian spouse says on the wedding day, "I will love you for better or for worse." This means unconditionally. When things really do get worse, this may not be much fun, but it is the only way human love can reflect divine love. And it is the only way to find happiness.

Loving God in this agapic way can be spoken of slightly differently from loving creatures. To love God as he commands is to give of ourselves to *please him* without conditions. Only what is truly good will please God.

There is something in this definition that should teach us the way to approach God. It should be *unconditional*. Sometimes we turn from God because he does not answer our prayers as we would like or allows terrible things to happen in our lives. But if we are to love in the way he has taught us—by his own example

—we should continue to pray without condition, especially the prayers of thanksgiving and adoration.

And if we are to love God, we must do so on *His terms*, not our own. Loving God on our terms is worth something, but it's like the six-year-old who gives a football to his mother. She smiles and considers the thought. But if he does the same when he's twenty-five, something is very wrong.

When we truly love people, we make every effort to discover what pleases them, what they really want. We love them *objectively*, not in some subjective way that pleases us. And what pleases God is not a great secret. It's easily found in Scripture and the Church's teachings, and it includes the Sunday Mass obligation and norms on sexuality.

There are other types of love that are more exciting, more stimulating. Emotional love, *eros*, the desire for the good, the beautiful and the true in the other, is thrilling but not divine. Friendship, *philia*, is very worthwhile and is at the heart of a good marriage, but it needs divine love to undergird it. Affection, *storge*, is a beautiful art that enriches lives, but without divine love it can become selfish.

It is *agape* that fulfills us and that often leads to intimacy. Jesus promised that it would involve a cross, that it would be hard, but he promised to lighten the load. There is no salvation without it.

Loving God

How do we love God? We begin the same way we begin to love others here on earth: by communication. No one can say they love God if they do not communicate with Him. This communication with God is called prayer. This is so important to our loving God that I have devoted several chapters to it in part two of this book.

We also love God by seeking His forgiveness in the sacrament of penance and by receiving His grace in each of the other sacraments. We love Him most powerfully by participating in the holy sacrifice of the Mass, the commemoration and reoffering of the sacrifice of Jesus on the cross. It is there that we participate in the "source and summit of the church's life and mission"[4] and "as from a font, grace is poured forth upon us" (*Sacrosanctum Concilium*, 10). There we find intimacy with Him.

It is one thing to love God, but to love Him with all our heart, soul, strength and mind, that's big. God doesn't expect us to keep holy His day only when we don't have shopping to do or a soccer game or party to attend. He expects us to arrange our Sunday—or our weekend if necessary—around the commitment to worship Him.

If we truly love God intensely, we will make our prayer life a priority as well. Even if we are just starting to pray and are only committed to five or ten minutes a day, we will plan our day around those few minutes. We will make sacrifices to be sure to complete our prayers. If we have to excuse ourselves from visiting friends or take the trouble to arrange a ride to church, so be it. When we're in love we find a way.

Granted, loving God may not at first involve the same emotional pull as being in love with someone on earth, but it should involve the same zeal. In one case the zeal is felt; in the other the zeal is willed. And happily, if we will the zeal for communicating with and worshiping God, in time we *will* feel it. *That* is the pearl of great price.

It is this sort of commitment that inspires a layperson to be able to say, "By the grace of God I've missed Sunday (or *daily*) Mass only five times in the last ten years, all for sickness," or a priest to be able to say, "By God's grace I have said Mass every day for thirty years." Archbishop Fulton Sheen said, "I have been blessed to make a Eucharistic holy hour every day for over fifty years."

Loving God with all our heart, soul, strength and mind is our first priority. And no one has ever regretted making this so.

. . . . .

The Life

of

Grace

CHAPTER FIVE

The Foundation: Prayer

At the end of World War II, the Russian army took over Austria. For three years they occupied that country, but then a priest by the name of Father Petrus began a rosary crusade. His goal was to get 10 percent of the Austrians, seven hundred thousand people, to pledge rosaries for deliverance from Russian rule, and he got it. After seven years of rosaries, on May 13, 1955,[1] inexplicably by human terms, the Russian army left Austria.[2] Prayer is a most powerful tool against evil!

Is prayer primarily about asking for what we want? No, but it certainly should include that. The Lord expects us to ask for things we need in prayer. In fact he said,

> Ask, and it will be given you; seek, and you will find; knock, and it
> will be opened to you. For every one who asks receives, and he
> who seeks finds, and to him who knocks it will be opened... If you
> then, who are evil, know how to give good gifts to your children,
> how much more will the heavenly Father give the Holy Spirit to
> those who ask him! (Luke 11:9–10, 13)

Prayer is our way of coming to know God and to love him. We come to God to thank him, to seek his forgiveness, to adore him and, yes, to ask for what we need. Indeed, prayer is the foundation of our entire life with the Lord.

What exactly is prayer? Prayer is simply lifting up the mind and heart to God. Or to put it differently, it is communicating with God. Saint Thérèse, the Little Flower, wrote, "For me, prayer is an upward leap of the heart, an untroubled glance towards heaven, a cry of gratitude and love which I utter from the depths of sorrow as well as from the heights of joy. It has a supernatural grandeur which expands the soul and unites it with God."[3]

Certainly adoration is the highest motive for prayer, but all four motives—adoration, contrition, thanksgiving and petition or supplication—should be practiced. The psalms, 150 songs addressed to God, are models for prayer, and they include all of the four motives.

Petition

We often find the psalmist petitioning or asking God for help. For example,

> Incline your ear to me,
>> rescue me speedily!
> Be a rock of refuge for me,
>> a strong fortress to save me!
>
> Yes, you are my rock and my fortress;
>> for your name's sake lead me and guide me. (Psalm 31:2–3)

Why does God encourage us to ask for things in prayer? For several reasons.

First, God wants us to be deeply aware that all good things come from Him. What better way than to invite us to seek His help in any need!

Second, God no doubt wants us to be humble enough to be aware of our neediness and to constantly realize that, no matter what spiritual heights we might reach, we are utterly dependent on Him for everything. Furthermore, God wants to manifest His presence and reward our faith by answering our prayers. This He does, sometimes in dramatic ways. This is a way of encouraging our faith. Many, many people have had their faith boosted by answers to prayer.

I met a young woman who was one of thirteen children, and virtually all of them attended Mass and prayed the rosary every day. I asked her to what she attributed this apparent faith among her brothers and sisters. She said that when they were young, they would all pray the rosary together as a family for special intentions, and their prayers were almost always answered. Thus, turning to God in time of need became a habit for them.

God wants us to get in the habit of communicating with Him. What better way than to appeal to one of our most basic instincts, our needs and desires?

Of course, we should understand *how* we are to ask for things and what we can expect. For example, Christ said: "If two of you agree on earth about anything they ask, it will be done for them by my Father in heaven" (Matthew 18:19). Would this include a prayer for the death of a business competitor? No. God, who is good, only grants good requests. That is why, at the end of any prayer in which we request something, we should add the words "if it be for my good" or "if it be Your will."

Thomas Merton began praying in earnest that he would have a novel he wrote accepted for publication. That novel was never accepted. But this began in Merton the habit of prayer, which was far more valuable than having a book published.

When I was a young man working as an engineer, I used to pray for relief from difficult love relationships. The Lord gave me relief, and in gratitude I continued praying hard, long after such relationships ended. As a result I found a relationship with God that has far exceeded the relationships I had been seeking.

Perhaps this little poem by an unknown Confederate soldier could help us understand how we pray and how God answers us.

> I asked for strength that I might achieve;
> I was made weak that I might learn humbly to obey.
> I asked for health that I might do greater things;
> I was given infirmity that I might do better things.
> I asked for riches that I might be happy;
> I was given poverty that I might be wise.
> I asked for power that I might have the praise of men;
> I was given weakness that I might feel the need of God.
> I asked for all things that I might enjoy life;
> I was given life that I might enjoy all things.
> I got nothing that I had asked for,
> but everything that I had hoped for.
> Almost despite myself my unspoken prayers were answered;
> I am, among all men, most richly blessed.[4]

It seems that if God does not give us what we ask for, He gives us something better. Saint Thérèse wrote, "I no longer know how to ask passionately for anything except that the will of God shall be perfectly accomplished in my soul."[5] This is what it means to really pray as a saint: to pray that the will of God shall be perfectly accomplished in our souls.

Thanksgiving

The motive of thanksgiving in prayer is extremely important. We are reminded to give thanks to God over forty times in the psalms. Psalm 136 is a good example. It begins with the verse, "O give thanks to the LORD, for he is good, / for his mercy endures for ever," and goes on for the next twenty-six verses to enumerate the reasons why we should give Him thanks.

When our Lord healed the ten lepers, He lamented the fact that only one returned to give thanks for his healing (see Luke 17:11–19). The word *thanks* appears fifty-eight times in the Old Testament, thirty-three times in the New; *thanksgiving* appears eighty-three and forty-eight times respectively.

We should be immensely thankful to God at every moment of every day. If we think clearly about our lives, most of us can find many, many things to thank Him for: for family, for friends, for intelligence, for health, for food and drink, for the beauty of the world, for our very existence. All of us have experienced at least some of these things.

I once worked with a young woman who was depressed. It was clear to me that she didn't have enough spiritual energy to pray the rosary daily, but she knew she needed to pray. I urged her to thank God for at least seven things every day and to be quite specific about just what those things were. She began to do so, and I believe she drew closer to God each day. She became more and more positive. After some months of that, the young woman overcame some of her depression and was able to pray the rosary daily. Since that time I have made every effort to take some of my own medicine and thank God all day long.

Some people have wonderful gifts, such as a good, faithful spouse, good children, good parents, good health, a good job, a holy pastor and any number of other good things—none of which they could claim to deserve—and they take them for granted. Then, when one of these is taken away, they become angry at God for letting them down. What ingratitude! Saint Paul asks, "What have you that you did not receive? If then you received it, why do you boast as if it were not a gift?" (1 Corinthians 4:7).

Do we really believe God owes us all these things? This is not to downplay the deep emotional hurt that often occurs when we lose someone or something very dear to us. But to be angry at God for the loss of one of His many gifts? Be sad, and ask for His consolation, but do not be angry. We should be thankful for the gifts we still have, especially our greatest gift, His friendship.

If God gave us nothing more than our existence and the *chance*, the *opportunity*, to learn to love Him and our neighbor, that we might experience the beauty and goodness of Love Himself in an eternal, intimate embrace, we would have reason to thank Him at every moment of our lives. If He never answered another prayer, we would still have reason to be grateful to Him for all eternity.

In the United States we have one day a year dedicated to thanksgiving. It's good that we have such a day, but every day should be a day to thank God for the many blessings He has given us. The Church celebrates "thanksgiving" every day: That is the meaning of the word *Eucharist*.

It would seem that thanking God always is an integral part of holiness. As the angel told Tobit and his father, "Praise God and give thanks to him; exalt him and give thanks to him in the presence of all the living for what he has done for you. It is good to praise God and to exalt his name, worthily declaring the works of God.... Do not be slow to give him thanks" (Tobit 12:6).

Contrition

Contrition, or sorrow for sins, is another motivation for prayer. Psalm 51 is a classic example of the prayer of contrition:

> Have mercy on me, O God,
>   according to your merciful love;
> according to your abundant mercy blot out my transgressions.

> Wash me thoroughly from my iniquity,
>> and cleanse me from my sin! (Psalm 51:1–2)

This psalm, also known as the *Miserere* or Prayer of Repentance, goes on for nineteen verses.

Saint John Vianney used to say near the end of his life that he wanted to retire from his pastorate and go to some monastery to weep for his sins. The holier we become, the more deeply we are aware of our sins.

Contrition is so important in our Church that we have a sacrament in which to express it (more about that in chapter ten). No doubt God knew our psychological need to alleviate our (reasonable) guilt, express our sorrow and seek forgiveness.

It seems that many people have lost a sense of sin, the awareness that we have done something wrong and need to change our ways. At the same time we sense that something is wrong. Could it be that we have…sinned?

We need not obsess over our sins, but we should have a healthy awareness of them. One way to accomplish that is to make a list of our three (or fewer) most prevalent sins, look at that list each night and pray an Act of Contrition before going to bed.

Adoration

Finally, adoration, the highest motive for prayer, is simply an outpouring of praise and love for God.

> Ascribe to the LORD, O sons of God,
>> ascribe to the LORD glory and strength.
> Ascribe to the LORD the glory of his name;
>> worship the LORD in holy attire. (Psalm 29:1–2)

(Incidentally, that last phrase, "worship the Lord in holy attire," is something we should remember as we dress for Sunday Mass.)

When you think of it, we have very little to offer God in return for His many wonderful gifts. He has *everything*, and yet we know that He delights in our words of praise and adoration. When we pray the prayer of adoration, He allows us to get closer to Him, to be His intimate lover.

Think of how praise affects you. When others praise you, don't you feel good? Don't you usually thank them for those words of praise? Don't you feel a bit closer to them? A child who receives much praise is likely to flourish and behave better and better. The person who often praises his or her spouse will often reap abundant rewards very quickly.

God does not need our praise, of course. He has all the self-confidence in the universe! But our praise and adoration please Him and move Him to bless us. And there is no limit to the things for which we can praise God: His kindness, His mercy, His beauty, His generosity, His wisdom, His glorious power, His infinite love.

We find some of the best prayers of adoration and praise in the psalms, the songs that were sung in the Jewish liturgy. Christ would have sung these as a child. They speak of the greatness of God, His mercy, His fidelity, His power, His goodness, His knowledge of all things past, present and future, His justice, His love for us. They show how small we are in comparison to Him and yet how He has given us great dignity and power. Psalm 8 is about the concern this magnificent God has for us, making us "little less than the angels."

The psalms tell us how to be happy: by following God's way. They remind us to call on God in difficult times: He will answer our prayers. They tell us that He is worthy of complete trust, that He is always near to us and concerned for us. He is our shepherd, guiding us through life toward His kingdom (Psalm 23, for example).

The psalms tell us that God's law is good and even delightful. They remind us that crime does not pay.

May we never tire of adoring God, of praising Him, of honoring Him. For He has given us every good thing we have and has invited us to be His spouse forever.

. . . . .

CHAPTER SIX

Beginning Prayer

Now, what are some of the methods of prayer?

Certainly one that is familiar to all is vocal prayer or formal prayer. In vocal prayer we follow a set formula, such as the Our Father or one of the psalms, and allow our hearts and minds to be lifted up to God through these words. "Vocal prayer, founded on the union of body and soul in human nature, associates the body with the interior prayer of the heart, following Christ's example of praying to his Father and teaching the Our Father to his disciples" (*CCC*, #2722).

The Psalms

Anyone who prays the psalms regularly will certainly know who God is and who we are. This is especially helpful for people who have had difficult fathers, for in the psalms we discover the true Father and the proper meaning of fatherhood.

Perhaps this is why the Church prescribes that priests and religious pray the psalms at least five times a day in the Divine Office, also known as the Liturgy of the Hours. Many laypeople also pray some portion of this.

There are five parts of the Liturgy of the Hours, plus two additional parts for members of contemplative orders:

1. Office of Readings: three psalms, a Scripture reading and a reading by or about a saint. This may be said the evening before or anytime during the day of prayer.

2. Morning Prayer (Lauds): three psalms, a reading, a response, the Gospel canticle (the *Benedictus* prayer or canticle of Zechariah upon the birth of his son, John the Baptist—Luke 1:68–79), petitions, the Our Father and a closing prayer.

3. Daytime Prayer: three psalms, a short reading, a brief response and a closing prayer. This is said around noon.

4. Evening Prayer (Vespers): same format as Morning Prayer, except that the Gospel canticle is the *Magnificat* (the humble prayer of Mary upon visiting Elizabeth—Luke 1:46–55).

5. Night Prayer (Compline): usually one psalm with a response, a short reading, a Gospel canticle (*Nunc Dimitis*, the prayer of Simeon upon seeing the Christ child at the presentation—Luke 2:29–32), a closing prayer and a hymn or prayer to Mary.

You need not pray the Divine Office to pray the psalms, but this is the official prayer of the Church, and thus using it means that you are praying with the whole Church.

The Our Father

Presumably most of us say the Our Father every day, but do we really know what it means, and do we think about what it means? Praying from the heart means knowing what you are saying and thinking about it when you pray. Anything less is a kind of thoughtless recitation of words, which is not as pleasing to God.

So what exactly does the Our Father mean?

The first word, *our*, should remind us that the Lord would have us pray with others. While private prayer is certainly important, Saint John Chrysostom taught, "[The Lord] teaches us to make prayer in common for all our brethren. For he did not say 'my

Father' who art in heaven, but 'our' Father, offering petitions for the common Body" (CCC, #2768, quoting *Homiliae in Matthaeum*, 19, 4: PG 57, 278).

In fact, Jesus is so pleased to see us pray together that He joins us: "Where two or three are gathered in my name, there am I in the midst of them" (Matthew 18:20). If Jesus prays with us, we shall certainly be heard!

The word *Father* reminds us of the intimacy God wishes to have with us. He is not merely King or Emperor or Teacher but our own Father. And He is the perfect Father. If we had an earthly father who was not so great, we can discover perfect fatherhood by getting to know God, especially in the psalms. We are His sons and daughters. He loves us passionately, unconditionally. He cares for us and has counted every hair on our heads (see Matthew 10:30; Luke 12:7).

"Who art in heaven, hallowed be Thy name." In other words, may Your name be held holy by all. We are asking not only that God's name be held holy but that the entire person of God be held holy, for in Scripture the term *name* refers to the person as a whole. The psalms speak of "calling on Your name," "glorifying Your name" and "loving Your name." When the apostles were beaten and told not to speak about Jesus by the Sanhedrin, they rejoiced that "they were counted worthy to suffer dishonor for the name" (Acts 5:41). So with these words we pray, "May your entire person be held holy by all."

"Thy kingdom come." By this phrase we are saying, Lord, may Your kingdom soon be fully established in me and in the hearts of all, so that we might live together in Your peace and love. Francis of Assisi and his friars brought the joy and peace of God's kingdom everywhere they went. In doing so they rekindled the fire of God's love in Europe and beyond.

"Thy will be done on earth as it is in heaven." This is a parallel phrase to the one just given. May we all do *and accept* Your will here on earth as it is done and accepted in heaven. This is one of the most difficult phrases in the Our Father, and it should never be spoken lightly. It involves surrendering our wills to God's will, be it pleasant or unpleasant.

When we lose a loved one, it is hard to say, "Thy will be done." In fact, a barometer of our love of God is our ability to say this sincerely in a time of intense sadness. We receive the cross Jesus promised us if we would follow Him. Mysteriously, our happiness is contained in the will of God, nowhere else.

What *is* God's will for us? That we become holy, "perfect," as Jesus said (Matthew 5:48). We should keep that in mind when we pray the Our Father.

"Give us this day our daily bread." *Bread* here refers to our needs. We ask God to supply them as He does for the birds of the air and the flowers of the fields. And if we pray this sincerely, we can be sure that God will indeed supply us with our true needs. The fathers of the Church also saw this bread as referring to the Bread of Life, the Eucharist, the food for our souls.

"And forgive us our trespasses as we forgive those who trespass against us." Here again is a difficult thing to say. May You forgive our sins, Lord, as we forgive others, even our enemies. In fact, this is the only passage in the Our Father upon which Jesus elaborates. He says, "[I]f you do not forgive [others] their trespasses, neither will your Father forgive your trespasses" (Matthew 6:15).

Forgiveness is a central trait of a true Christian. When we think of the many sins God forgives us, it is a mere pittance for us to forgive even the most grievous injustices we have received. And forgiveness yields tangible good in the here and now. For example, our chances of getting heart disease or cancer are considerably reduced if we forgive others.[1]

"And lead us not into temptation." That is, keep us not only from sin but from the very situations where sin is appealing. Anyone who truly loves another will not only avoid sinning against that person but also stay far from situations that might lead to sin. We pray to be delivered from temptation, but we must do our part to accept God's grace to avoid it. How many young men and women seek forgiveness for their sins of the flesh yet go back to the same situations that have led to those sins?

"But deliver us from evil." That is, Lord, deliver us from the evil one. Let us never be under his spell in any way.

"Amen." Let it be so.

Notice, this beautiful prayer, sometimes called the "perfect prayer," includes three of the four motives for prayer. Adoration is behind the words "hallowed be Thy name"; supplication is found throughout the prayer (for example, "Give us this day our daily bread"); and contrition is the motive in "forgive us our trespasses." We should pray the Our Father often, slowly meditating on the meaning of these beautiful words.

Saint Teresa of Avila wrote a long meditation on the Our Father. At one point she wrote, "To keep you from thinking that little is gained through a perfect recitation of vocal prayer, I tell you that it is very possible that while you are reciting the Our Father or some other vocal prayer, the Lord may raise you to perfect contemplation."[2]

Talking With God

Another, less formal method of prayer is simply to speak to God in our own words, telling Him of our troubles, our joys, our needs and our desires. This is typically called conversation.

The more we pray, the more comfortable we feel talking to God during our day. Ours is a personal God. Jesus told us that He has counted every hair on our head (see Luke 12:7). He cares about everything we do. We should enjoy speaking to Him all day long, knowing how close He is to us.

There are scores of things each day that we can thank God for, such as the weather, our health, the blessing of food, our family and friends. Every good thing we experience should remind us to thank God. And of course, we should feel comfortable asking God for what we need, adding the condition, "if it be for my good and according to Your will."

We can praise God with a daylong outpouring of love and joy in the Lord for everything that happens in our life, good or bad. Especially bad. Why? Because as Merlin Carothers points out in his book *Prison to Praise*, Romans 8 tells us, "We know that in everything God works for good with those who love him" (Romans 8:28). To praise God for even the apparently bad things that happen is to trust Him, and God loves trust. He told Saint Maria Faustina, "The graces of My mercy are drawn by means of one vessel only, and that is—trust. The more a soul trusts, the more it will receive. Souls that trust boundlessly are a great comfort to Me, because I pour all the treasures of My graces into them."[3] He also told her, "Sins of distrust wound Me most painfully."[4]

Charismatic prayer is very much about praising God—in tongues, in words, in gestures. Charismatic prayer and the charisms are based on 1 Corinthians 14:1–5 and other passages from First Corinthians. Many have benefitted greatly from their involvement in charismatic prayer groups.

This brings us back to the topic of community prayer. Is it better to pray alone or with others?

Our natural inclination may be to pray alone, but as I said earlier, the Lord encouraged us to pray with others: "For where two or three are gathered in my name, there am I in the midst of them" (Matthew 18:20). Saint John Vianney said, "Private prayer resembles straw scattered here and there over a field; if it is set on fire, the flame is not a powerful one; but if you gather those scattered straws into a bundle, the flame is bright, and rises in a lofty column towards the sky: such is public prayer."[5] (Jesus stated that we should go to our room, shut the door and pray [Matthew 6:6] in the context of avoiding praying in public to be seen.)

Perhaps we have all thought, as I have, "I could pray the rosary much faster saying it alone than saying it with the parishioners after Mass." However, we must remember that although it takes more time, we receive far more grace by saying it with others. Even if it took twice as long, it would be worth it, since we might speculate that it could be three or four times as beneficial.

Certainly anyone who prays much will do a lot of private prayer. Nonetheless, as Saint Francis de Sales mentioned, "God has ordained that communion of prayers should always have preference to every kind of private prayer."[6]

. . . . .

CHAPTER SEVEN

Spiritual Reading

It has been said that prayer that doesn't change us just isn't prayer. But how does change come?

The answer lies in spiritual reading. By reading the Scriptures and the lives and writings of the saints and other holy men and women, we discover what we ought to do in order to become holy. Saint Jerome said, "When we pray we speak to God; but when we read [spiritual books], God speaks to us."[1] Saint Francis de Sales wrote, "You should...read stories and lives of the saints for there, as in a mirror, you can see a picture of the Christian life and adapt their deeds to your use in keeping with your vocation."[2]

How much spiritual reading should we do each day? For most people a good beginning would be about five pages a day. Eventually ten pages a day would be reasonable to sustain a strong spiritual life. That doesn't seem like much, but that's 3,650 pages a year.

We should remember that spiritual reading is not like recreational reading. The latter is done for enjoyment, whereas spiritual reading is done for formation.

It's important that we not do too much spiritual reading at a time, especially if we find a particularly interesting book. We can become what we might call a "spiritual glutton," as one of my friends in the seminary did. He would find a good book on a saint and read it in just a few days. Then he would have a great letdown when the next book was not so interesting. Best to read just a small amount each day, so that "dry" reading—and some of the best spiritual books are dry and difficult to read—will be bearable, and interesting books will not move us to spend too much time reading to the neglect of our prayer or work.

We should find a good time to do spiritual reading. In the seminary nighttime reading proved best for me, just before bed. However, once I got involved in a parish, I was too tired to read at night. So I moved reading to the morning, after prayer but before I did any work for the day. Each person must discover the best time for him or her and then exercise self-discipline to develop the habit of reading daily.

Scripture should always take first place in spiritual reading. Scripture is very rich; reading it should be limited to a maximum of one chapter a day. The lives of the saints, to be sure, have a special relation to Scripture. Saint Francis de Sales wrote, "There is no more difference between the Gospel written and the life of a saint than between music written and music sung."[3]

There are a hundred other things we must develop in order to draw close to God in love: things such as devotion to Mary and the Sacred Heart of Jesus; loving the Church, the pope and the teachings of the Church; delighting in the Mass and the sacrament of the Eucharist; being willing to suffer for Christ. The only way to develop a deep and truly Catholic sense of these things is to read the lives and the writings of the saints. By reading a little each day, you will be stirred to a real fervor for the things of God, and you will avoid the many pitfalls in the spiritual journey. This is the most effective (and enjoyable) way to maintain growth in holiness.

There are a handful of books that have changed many lives. Here are five:

1. *St. Francis of Assisi* by Omer Englebert
2. *The Story of a Soul*, by Saint Thérèse of Lisieux
3. *St. Teresa of Ávila* by Marcelle Auclair
4. *Our Lady of Fatima* by William Thomas Walsh
5. *Introduction to the Devout Life* by Saint Francis de Sales

If you do not have a Catholic bookstore nearby, you can order these books online at Amazon.com. You can also get them used, at greatly reduced prices, from Half.com or Amazon.com.[4]

Notice that only the last of these books is a philosophical book about holiness (and by the way, it is *the* classic on the spiritual life). All the others are biographical. Whenever I give direction to people who read many philosophical books, I encourage them to always get back to a biography, because these seem to be far more effective in bringing about conversion. The things that the saints did are often easier to remember than the things they wrote. In reading a biography of a saint, our defenses against changing or doing more for God are bypassed, since the saints do not ask us to do more: They simply show us by example. Each time you read a book on a saint, you will undergo at least a small conversion.

Are anthologies of saints worthwhile? Although they can be useful, entire books about one saint will generally give you more insight into a person's life and will prove more inspiring. Just a few pages of reading each day will enable you to learn from a saint how to become a saint.

Just about all the saints read lives of the saints. Saint Thérèse of Lisieux wrote, "I love to read the lives of the saints...; the account of their heroic deeds inflames my courage and spurs me on to imitate them."[5] Saint Athanasius said, "You will not see anyone who is really striving after his advancement who is not given to spiritual reading, and to him who neglects it, the fact will soon be observed in his [lack of] progress."[6]

It should be noted that although spiritual reading is closely linked to prayer and provides a strong incentive to pray more, it is not prayer. If there is a choice between prayer and reading (a rare situation, I hope), prayer should take precedence. I encourage you to pray before reading, since prayer opens our hearts to spiritual reading.

All the saints were into one of the most powerful types of prayer, meditation. This involves reading and thinking about the Word of God, about an event in the life of Christ or some attribute of God. Sometimes called "mental prayer," this is considered a richer type of prayer than vocal prayer or conversation with God. We will dedicate the next chapter to meditative prayer and to contemplative prayer (something God works in us).

. . . . .

CHAPTER EIGHT

Meditation and Contemplation

According to the Catholic Catechism, "Meditation is a prayerful quest engaging thought, imagination, emotion, and desire. Its goal is to make our own in faith the subject considered, by confronting it with the reality of our own life" (CCC, #2723). To put it more simply, meditation is simply thinking in a focused way about something of God, especially an aspect of the life of Christ. Meditation is sometimes called "mental prayer."

An example of meditation is *lectio divina*, literally "divine reading" (of Scripture, usually, or another classic spiritual work, such as *The Imitation of Christ* by Thomas à Kempis). I recommend the Gospels as a wonderful source.

In *lectio divina* you read a passage until you come across something that grabs your attention. (I do not recommend reading genealogies for this!) Then you ponder the meaning of the text, opening your heart to receive the message God has for you, seeking to embrace it intuitively in love and adoration. Finally you allow yourself to rejoice in the gift of God's presence and consider a way in which you can apply this to your life and grow in virtue.[1]

Other methods of meditation are the rosary and the Stations of the Cross. In both of these the meditations come once again from the Scriptures. I have dedicated the entire next section to the rosary, as it is an important prayer of the Church.

Although the Stations of the Cross are most often prayed on the Fridays of Lent, some people, including myself, pray them every day. [2] Christ said to Saint Faustina Kowalska, "There is more merit to one hour of meditation on My sorrowful Passion than there is to a whole year of flagellation that draws blood."[3]

Meditation is considered the highest form of active prayer (contemplation being more receptive than active), perhaps because it is a way of allowing God to speak to us through His Word or through the life of Christ. So often when we pray we do all the talking, and God can hardly get a word in edgewise. When we meditate we listen to God and allow His words to sink deep into our subconscious. We should remember that God has given us only one mouth but two ears!

Meditating on the Rosary

The rosary is meant to be a meditation on twenty mysteries of Christ's and Mary's lives, with the Hail Marys as gentle "background music" to accompany the meditation and measure time. In fact, it is recommended while praying a mystery that one think only about the mystery and not concentrate on the words of the Hail Mary at all. The recitation of the rosary is the only instance when you would say a vocal prayer and not think about the words you are saying.

There are many advantages to praying the rosary. The twenty mysteries focus on the central events of our faith and are based on Sacred Scripture. Each mystery can be found either literally or figuratively in Scripture, and each portrays an important happening in the life of Jesus or His mother. Once the meditations are learned, using Sacred Scripture as a guide or a booklet[4] of meditations published for this purpose, the rosary can be said anywhere and anytime: while driving a car, in a crowded airport or on a bus or train. For discretion or convenience, a rosary that fits on the finger like a ring may be used.

The rosary can be said alone or with others, since it is one of the few meditative prayers that lend themselves easily to group prayer. The rosary beads running through one's fingers are a psychological aid to concentration. The rosary can be recited in three-minute segments, since each decade stands on its own. This makes it ideal as an introductory prayer for young children or busy adults, who may think it too much to pray five mysteries at a time. Two or three mysteries a day make a good beginning, and the five mysteries of one rosary may eventually be spread out over the course of a day.

Parents can use pictures and tell the story of a particular mystery before and after praying with their children. This makes prayer more interesting and provides a learning experience for the children as well. Children are often delighted with the stories and are eager to learn more.

Another advantage to the rosary is that it contains the essential mysteries of our faith and thus leads us into the Mass, "the source and the summit of the Christian life" (*Lumen Gentium*, 11). The rosary includes the Apostles' Creed, the statement of our faith, and the Our Father, the perfect prayer. The twenty different mysteries provide variety for meditation. Each decade is concluded with "Glory be to the Father," in praise of the Blessed Trinity, and the Fatima prayer, "O my Jesus, forgive us our sins. Save us from the fires of hell, especially those in most need of Thy mercy."

If your mind wanders off to some unrelated topic during private recitation of the rosary, you may repeat some Hail Marys.

This is a way to teach yourself the discipline of concentration.

Finally, the rosary allows you to meditate at several different levels. You may simply meditate on the event of the mystery, on its basic theme or on the virtue suggested by the event (some call the latter the "fruit" of the mystery).

Another way of meditating with the rosary is one suggested by Saint Louis de Montfort and Popes Paul VI and John Paul II. You add a descriptive phrase after the word *Jesus* in the Hail Mary. The following are based in part on Saint Louis's suggestions[5]:

THE MYSTERIES OF
THE ROSARY

Joyful

1 - Jesus incarnate

2 - Jesus sanctifying

3 - Jesus born in poverty

4 - Jesus acclaimed

5 - Jesus lost and found

Sorrowful

1 - Jesus in agony

2 - Jesus scourged

3 - Jesus crowned with thorns

4 - Jesus carrying his cross

5 - Jesus crucified

Glorious

1 - Jesus risen from the dead

2 - Jesus ascending

3 - Jesus sending the Spirit

4 - Jesus assuming you

5 - Jesus crowning you

Luminous (new in 2003)

1 - Jesus baptized

2 - Jesus who worked a
       miracle at Cana

3 - Jesus who proclaimed the
       kingdom

4 - Jesus transfigured

5 - Jesus our Eucharist

So the rosary is a meditative prayer, not simply the mindless repetition of Hail Marys that some of our separated brethren believe it to be. In fact, some Protestants have come to appreciate the value of the rosary. Richard Bauman, a German Lutheran minister, said:

> In saying the rosary, truth sinks into the subconscious like a slow and heavy downpour. The hammered sentences of the Gospel receive an indelible validity for precisely the little ones, the least, to whom belongs the Kingdom of Heaven.... The rosary is a long and persevering gaze, a meditation, a quieting of the spirit in praise of God, the value of which we Protestants are learning more and more.[6]

According to *Soul* magazine in March–April 1990, the divorce rate for couples praying the rosary together every day was one in five hundred, as compared to the national average of one in two. Thus it is no wonder that Popes John Paul II and Paul VI wrote,

> We now desire, as a continuation of the thought of our predecessors, to recommend strongly the recitation of the family rosary.... There is no doubt that...the rosary should be considered as one of the best and most efficacious prayers in common that the Christian family is invited to recite. We like to think and sincerely hope that when the family gathering becomes a time of prayer the rosary is a frequent and favored manner of praying.[7]

Pope John Paul II called the rosary his favorite prayer, and he said, "Pray, pray much. Say the Rosary every day." An earlier pope, Benedict XV, wrote, "The prayer of the Rosary is perfect because of the praises it offers, the lessons it teaches, the graces it obtains, and the victories it achieves."[8]

Mary appeared at Fatima on May 13, 1917, and said to Lucia, Francisco and Jacinta, "Say the Rosary every day, to obtain peace for the world, and the end of the war." On July 13 she reiterated, "[C]ontinue to say five decades of the Rosary every day in honor of Our Lady of the Rosary to obtain the peace of the world and the end of the war.... If [people] do what I tell you, many souls will be saved, and there will be peace."[9]

Do we want world peace?

Contemplation

The *Catechism* defines contemplation: "Contemplative prayer is the simple expression of the mystery of prayer. It is a gaze of faith fixed on Jesus, an attentiveness to the Word of God, a silent love. It achieves real union with the prayer of Christ to the extent that it makes us share in his mystery" (CCC, #2724).

Father Thomas Dubay elaborates: "Christic contemplation is nothing less than a deep love communion with the triune God.... It is not merely a mentally expressed 'I love You.' It is a wordless awareness and love that we of ourselves cannot initiate or prolong."[10]

We read in the First Letter of John: "Whoever confesses that Jesus is the Son of God, God abides in him, and he in God. So we know and believe the love God has for us. God is love, and he who abides in love abides in God, and God abides in him" (1 John 4:15–16). It is this mutual abiding or dwelling within each other that constitutes contemplative prayer.

Contemplative prayer is not something we can produce: it is entirely God's initiative. Teresa of Ávila said she could not produce the first "spark" of this fire of God's love that penetrated her; it was all His doing.[11] She pointed out that although this prayer was filled with delight, this delight should not be something we seek; rather we should seek to share in the cross of Christ.[12]

Father Dubay states that our life of virtue must grow if we wish to be able to grow in contemplation. "[I]f humility, patience, temperance, chastity and love for neighbor are not growing, neither is prayer growing."[13] And he adds that there are many different levels of contemplation.[14]

Thus, although this sort of prayer depends totally on the initiative of God, we can prepare ourselves for it. The purpose of this book is to help us prepare for this intimacy.

. . . . .

CHAPTER NINE

Difficulties in Prayer

Some people claim that they have so many distractions in prayer, they get discouraged. Some say prayer is just too boring. Others lose heart when the good feelings, the "consolations" they used to get, disappear. Still others have told me, "I don't have time for prayer. I am too busy."

Not to worry. There's a solution for each of these.

Is Prayer Boring?

Of course prayer is boring—at first. Many things are boring at first. Take school for starters. As time goes on and we begin to develop a base of knowledge, it becomes more interesting, but it's very boring at first. Most people persevere in studying because they want to become educated and get a well-paying job.

Sports can be boring in the early stages. When I went out for the track team in high school, all we did was exercises for the first two weeks. Only after that did I get to do what I came for, high-jumping and pole-vaulting. Football is the same. In both college and pro there is no football for several weeks in training camp, only boring, hard workouts. The players lift weights all during the off-season. That, too, is boring.

Most jobs are boring at first. We persevere because we are getting paid.

Suppose we decided to just do things that were stimulating. No more boring activities: no school, no organized sports, no chores at home, no jobs. Just lots of television, computer games and other games. We'd end up in jail!

Think of all the things in life that have made you a better person: studying, training for sports, helping others, working. All boring at first but all enriching.

So is prayer—early on. Were we expecting a party to get to the kingdom?

Isn't it interesting that we are willing to endure some boredom to get an education, to earn money, or to train for a sports team, but we fear boredom when it comes to thanking God for creating and sustaining us and for giving us every good thing simply so He could share with us His happiness? Sunday Mass? Prayer? Too boring!

Jesus Himself promised a cross for those who would follow him. He said, "If any man would come after me, let him deny himself and take up his cross daily and follow me. For whoever would save his life will lose it; and whoever loses his life for my sake, he will save it" (Luke 9:23–24). Some apparently think that boredom mustn't be included in that cross. Boredom in prayer can indeed be the first cross of a Christian.

Saint Teresa of Ávila was often extremely bored by prayer. She could feel so miserable when it was time to enter the chapel for meditative prayer that she had to force herself to go in and could hardly wait for the hour to be up. Nonetheless, after she made herself do this, she often felt better about the prayer she had done than when she felt like praying![1]

Later Teresa wrote that when she abandoned prayer, it was no more than "putting myself right in hell without the need of devils."[2] For "there is but one road which reaches God and that is prayer; if anyone shows you another, you are being deceived."[3]

This transformation of Teresa is typical of many who begin to pray. It is extremely difficult at first to get into the habit, but once a person has gotten through that difficulty, they begin to love prayer, especially when they see what it does for them.

Distractions

Should we worry about distractions in prayer? No. Everyone has distractions, even saints. Saint Thérèse explained to a novice: "I also have many [distractions], but as soon as I am aware of them, I pray for those people the thought of whom is diverting my attention, and in this way they reap benefit from my distractions."[4]

According to a legend told by Bishop Sheen, Saint Bernard was out riding with a friend when he began lamenting his distractions in prayer. His friend remarked that he was never distracted. Bernard found that hard to believe. He offered to give his friend his horse if the friend could kneel down right there and say one Our Father without a single distraction.

His companion accepted the challenge. He dismounted, knelt down and began to pray out loud. When he got to the words "give us this day our daily bread," he stopped, looked up at Saint Bernard and asked, "Do I get the saddle too?" Bernard kept his horse!

We should not be surprised if we are distracted in prayer. As soon as we become aware of distractions, we need only bring our minds back to God and try again to keep them focused on the subject of our meditation. When praying the rosary we may avoid distractions by using one of the many booklets that contain meditations on each mystery.[5] Or if we're riding in a car, we might play a recording of meditations on the rosary.[6]

Saint Teresa of Ávila found herself very distracted one day after receiving Holy Communion. She began to envy those living in the desert without any distractions. She heard the voice of the Lord: "You are greatly mistaken, daughter; rather, the temptations of the devil there are stronger; be patient, for as long as you live, a wandering mind cannot be avoided."[7]

Dryness in Prayer

How often people say to me that they don't think they are praying as effectively as they ought. I like to remind them of these
words of Saint Teresa of Ávila: "The Lord doesn't look so much
at the greatness of our works as at the love with which they are
done."[8] Saint Francis de Sales wrote, "We should labor without
any uneasiness as to results. God requires efforts on our part, but
not success."[9]

Some people say their prayer doesn't seem to "go anywhere."
They don't get that wonderful feeling they used to get in prayer.
This should never worry us. At times we all have what is called
"dryness" in prayer, or prayer with no consolations. Unfortunately
some individuals withdraw from prayer when this happens. But this
is wrong. We should pray all the harder when everything is dry,
knowing that we receive that much more grace when we do.

Saint Francis de Sales wrote regarding prayer: "If [God] con-
soles me I kiss the right hand of His mercy; If I am dry and distracted, I kiss the left hand of His justice."[10] And Saint Thérèse
said that she could expect heaven because she prayed when all
seemed dark and arid.

Why does God permit us to suffer dryness in prayer? Why
doesn't He reward us with consolations every time we pray?

In withdrawing consolations God is asking us, "Do you love
Me or My consolations?" He wants to see if we will love Him as
spouses promise to love, "in good times and in bad." Saint Francis
de Sales tells us to seek not the consolations of God but the God
of all consolations.

Unanswered Prayer

Sometimes we find prayer difficult because it seems that God
doesn't answer us. But in fact, often when we pray for a specific
favor from the Lord, we fail to notice that he has answered us.

The story is told of the man, already late for an important meeting, who was looking for a parking space. He prayed, "Lord, if you find me a space, I will pray the rosary every day."

Alas, no space was forthcoming. He prayed further, "Lord, if you find me a space, I will give up drinking."

Immediately someone pulled out, and he got his space. He said, "Nevermind, Lord. I found a space myself."

Then there was the man who stayed with his house during a flood. As the waters rose he climbed up on the roof. Some people came by in a rowboat and offered him a ride to safety, but he told them, "No, thanks. I have prayed to God, and he will save me."

Shortly thereafter, as his space on the roof shrank, a man in a motorboat offered him a saving ride, but his reply was the same. Finally, as he clung to the top of the chimney with the water swirling around, someone offered him a rope from a helicopter, but he again declined, saying, "God will save me."

Finally the man was swept away in the floodwater, and he drowned. When he met the Lord, he complained, "Lord, you disappointed me. I prayed that you would save me, and I ended up drowning. What happened?"

The Lord answered him, "I sent three different people to save you, and you turned them all down."

How important it is to realize that the way God answers our prayers is often by sending someone to give us what we need. And how important it is that we thank Him.

One of the most common difficulties that people express about prayer is finding time for it. This, I find, is mostly a question of commitment. We'll talk about that in the next chapter.

. . . . .

CHAPTER TEN

Commitment to Prayer

How much time should we spend each day in prayer? Naturally this depends on our age, our state in life and a number of other factors, but perhaps we might try to establish some averages.

For someone leading a busy life who has never prayed more than two or three short prayers at morning and night, I usually recommend a commitment of at least five minutes a day of meditation. That's not much time, but to do this amount of prayer each day for several months is to begin the way of holiness. Anyone who claims to be too busy for this has no concept of what he or she owes God in gratitude for all His gifts. Such a person is asking for trouble, eternal trouble.

Saint Teresa of Ávila wrote, "It is essential to begin the practice of prayer with a firm resolution of persevering in it."[1] It's easier to go from five minutes a day to fifteen minutes a day than to go from a couple of short prayers to five minutes of meditation daily. Anyone who prays comes to realize that, as Saint John Vianney said, "the more we pray, the more we wish to pray."[2]

Of course, the opposite is true as well: The less you pray the less you want to pray. As we continue to pray, no matter how hard we find it at first, it becomes easier. Perhaps the great miracle in anyone's life is their first commitment to pray.

Getting Started

Beginning to pray can be a great trial for a modern man or woman. We are so busy making money, studying and having fun that we find it difficult to stop all that, quiet our senses and pray to God in silence. We can't see God, we can't touch Him, we can't hear Him the way we hear others, and we're not sure He hears us or answers us.

And yet we must communicate with Him in order to fulfill his greatest commandment, to love Him. Saint Alphonsus de Liguori said, "Those who pray are certainly saved; those who do not pray are certainly damned" (CCC, #2744, quoting *Del gran mezzo della preghiera*).

So to begin this communication is of utmost importance. We need not be elegant about it or follow any defined structures at first. We don't have to pray before the Blessed Sacrament, even though that is the best place to pray, and we don't have to pray on our knees at first.

I began to pray in bed at night, and because it often took a half hour for me to get to sleep, I usually finished five mysteries of the rosary nightly. That was my first commitment to pray, and to that foundation I attribute every good thing that followed in my life. My mother used to say that if I fell asleep before finishing the rosary, my angel would finish it for me. That's not dogma, but I am willing to bet that it's true.

Imagine if we could get every person to use all their time waiting to fall asleep for prayer. What a beautiful world we would have!

What else do we do with this time? Waste it, mostly. Perhaps we ponder our work or how we will win the heart of a new love, but in fact, thinking about such things tends to keep us awake, while praying tends to quiet us better for sleep. Some count sheep to help them sleep. How much better to pray to the Lamb!

One mother told her daughter not to pray in bed. She felt it wasn't respectful to fall asleep while communicating with the Lord. But look at it this way: How beautiful it is to share our final words and thoughts each day with our Lord. And how beautiful to spend fifteen minutes or more each day in prayer to God, which we might not otherwise spend with Him.

What a great way to encourage people who think they're too busy to pray. I often poll young people on this, and invariably a large majority raise their hands when I ask who takes fifteen or more minutes to get to sleep.

Now, what about those who fall asleep within minutes of hitting the pillow? What a blessing! Had I had such a gift, I would willingly kneel by the bed and pray fifteen minutes a night *at least* in gratitude.

Young mothers can pray as they rest in bed while their children nap in the afternoon. Or they can pray out loud with their children, even those who are too young to understand prayer. Many people pray while they are driving or walking. Some pray while they are waiting in line at the grocery store. My mother used to pray during the commercials while watching television.

Isn't that disrespectful, watching TV while praying? There's a story of two religious discussing whether they should do this. They couldn't come to a conclusion, so each wrote to Rome for an answer.

The first wrote asking if it was OK to watch television while praying, and the answer came back, "Absolutely not."

The second wrote asking if it was OK to pray while watching TV. The answer he got was, "Yes, that's fine."

Sure, dedicated prayer on your knees before the Blessed Sacrament is best, but you needn't start with that. Sure, it's better to pray the Sorrowful Mysteries of the rosary on Tuesday and Friday, on rosary beads, but if you don't know which days to do which mysteries, and you don't have rosary beads handy, pray any mysteries, and use your fingers. Start doing the best you can, and later on you can refine things. Don't let anything stop you from getting into prayer.

Growing in Prayer

Once a person has made prayer a daily habit, he or she ought to try to slowly increase the time. Many have discovered that the more generous they are with God in prayer, the more efficient He will make them in their work. Blessed Mother Teresa of Calcutta used to say that if we pray, we can do twice as much in less time because we are not doing it; God is.

Our growth in prayer should be steady, not advancing too quickly, so as to become burdensome, and not settling into a rut at a certain level. Bishop Fulton Sheen used to say in his retreats that there are no plains in the spiritual life. We are either going uphill, or we are going down. If we are the same as we were last year, we are worse, for the spiritual life was meant to grow.

How do we know if we are praying enough? I believe our prayers should make us a bit uncomfortable but not burdened. If we find it comfortable, we are probably not praying enough, and it is time to grow. If we feel burdened by our prayer commit-ment, we are probably trying to grow too quickly. It is impossi-ble to become a saint overnight.

Prayer is like lifting weights. If you go into the weight room and put a light weight on the bar and keep lifting that, you will never get strong. If, on the other hand, you put too much weight on the bar, you may hurt yourself, or you may become quite dis-couraged and give up. But if you do things properly, you will start with a weight that challenges you, something you can lift but not easily. As you get stronger, you add more weight every few weeks, and you keep getting stronger.

As you grow in prayer, your relationship with God keeps getting stronger, and you are better able to overcome sin and become holy and virtuous.

In terms of time, what sort of goal should we have for prayer?

Although we don't find the answer directly in Scripture, I think it's there indirectly. In the Old Testament we see that Abraham gave a tenth of everything to Melchizedek, the priest of God Most High, who was a Christ figure (see Genesis 14:18–20). The Lord commanded the Israelites to tithe, giving 10 percent of their goods to the Levites, who were in turn to give 10 percent of what they received to the Lord (see Numbers 18:21–24). If the Israelites gave 10 percent of their goods, could we not give 10 percent of both our goods and our time to the Lord? Ten percent of our waking hours for most of us is a little more than an hour and a half each day. That might seem like a lot, but considering that we have perhaps forty to fifty years to get to that level, it should be a reasonable goal.

The Habit of Prayer

When I was a young boy, I was convinced there was only one kind of habit: bad. That was the only type I seemed to have. Then, after fourteen cavities and many unpleasant visits to the dentist, I developed my first good habit: brushing my teeth. From that tender age I began to brush my teeth daily, and I never gave it another thought. I never asked myself if I was going to brush my teeth; I just did it.

So it should be with prayer. We should develop a habit of prayer, such that we just do it each day, without question.

Granted, because of schedule changes, we may have to move our prayer time here and there during the day, but if we consider it a priority, we will rearrange our schedule to make sure we do it. The things we really want to get done, we schedule as early as possible in the day. This is not to say that we won't pray late in the day, but most of our prayer should be done before 9 PM, so that we are wide awake and give God our best hours. For many people this might mean right after dinner.

Isn't this a contradiction to what we already said about praying in bed? No, because praying in bed is meant as an incentive for those who are just beginning prayer and who might think themselves too busy to set aside time for it during the day. If our commitment is just fifteen minutes a day of prayer, praying in bed might cover it. However, when we begin to pray half an hour daily and more, much of that should be done long before bedtime. We should never give God just the dregs of our day. Of course we should pray before we retire for the night, but that need only be something brief—an examination of conscience and an Act of Contrition—if we have prayed during the day.

One very important ingredient for good prayer is silence. Alas, there is very little silence in the Western world, with our televisions, iPods, cell phones and so on. But to really get close to God we must put all that aside. We should take care to leave the television and radio off in the morning, in order to begin our day thinking about Him and praising Him.

Saint Alphonsus Ligouri said, "Prayer is a necessary means of salvation without which we cannot remain in the grace of God. The damned have been damned because they did not pray; the saints have become saints because they did pray."[3] Prayer is our most fundamental way of loving God; without it we lose our very connection with God, our faith will die, and our soul will shrivel up like a dead flower. With prayer we blossom day after day with the very life of God. We can show God to the world!

Pray, Pray, Pray!

We read in First Thessalonians: "Rejoice always, pray constantly, give thanks in all circumstances; for this is the will of God in Christ Jesus for you" (1 Thessalonians 5:16–18). Jesus told the disciples the parable of the corrupt judge, who cared little about justice but responded to the widow's pleas because she was persistent. He promised that God would answer those who "cry out to him day and night." The point was "that they ought always to pray and not lose heart" (Luke 18:1).

Our blessed Lord told Peter on the night he betrayed Him, "Watch and pray that you may not enter into temptation" (Matthew 26:41). Bishop Sheen commented that after having denied Christ three times and enduring such anguish over this betrayal, Peter must have wished that he had "watched and prayed."

The word *pray* appears 72 times in the Old Testament, 76 in the New; the word *prayed*, 64 and 20; and the word *prayer*, 197 and 126.

The Gospel of Luke is known as the Gospel of prayer. Luke shows Jesus praying at key times in His life: at His baptism (3:21); before He chose the apostles (6:12); before Peter declared Him the Christ (9:18); before the Transfiguration (9:28); when He taught the disciples to pray (11:1); at the Last Supper (22:32); the night before He died (22:41) and finally on the cross (23:46). Luke also tells us that Jesus would go off to quiet places to pray (5:16), and He warned the apostles to "pray that you may not enter into temptation" (22:40). Prayer should be in our blood!

Saint Ignatius was always at prayer. Francis of Assisi spent long hours praying, and it was during one of his extended periods of prayer that he received the stigmata. When Saints Clare and

John of the Cross came from prayer, their faces glowed. Saint John of the Cross wrote, "Do not omit mental prayer for any occupation, for it is the sustenance of your soul."[4] And Father Henri Nouwen wrote that reminding people to pray was like reminding them to breathe!

To those who tell me they have a great deal of trouble getting into prayer, I suggest simply thanking God all day long for the good things in their lives. Those who have done so often begin to pray more formally in time. Another approach that has brought success is to start with one Hail Mary daily, asking Our Lady to help you grow in prayer. That's a prayer she'll answer!

. . . . .

CHAPTER ELEVEN

The Sacrament of Penance

A young man once gave a talk about his conversion. He had been a Catholic since childhood but fell into sin and neglected confession, though he continued to go to Mass. So he did need conversion.

The young man went to confess one Saturday afternoon and found himself at the end of a long line of people. He looked at his watch and decided he didn't have time. He started to leave, a bit relieved that he could put this confession off some more.

A woman close to the confessional grabbed the young man as he went by and said, "Here, take my place. You look like you may need it more than I." Indeed he did. He was caught—by the Hound of Heaven. He went in and confessed for the first time in over ten years. He went on to become a very good priest.

The point of this story is that this man's conversion was centered on one event: his going to confession after many, many years. This was the key to his changing his life and surrendering to God.

So often confession is the beginning of a great conversion. Bishop Sheen told the story of Charles de Foucauld, who had some questions about the faith. He was directed to a Father Huvelin, who was in the confessional at the time. He told the priest he wanted to ask him some questions. The priest invited him to confess his sins. After some discussion back and forth, Charles did what the priest had asked. That was the day de Foucald converted.

Later he was ordained a priest, and he became a hermit in the Sahara Desert. He was beatified in 2005 by Pope Benedict XVI.

Frequent Confession

There is a vast difference spiritually between those who go to confession regularly—once a month—and those who do not. Confession has a way of making us more honest about ourselves and our relationship with God.

A man once went on retreat, and when he told the retreat director in confession that he hadn't confessed in several years, the priest warned him of the danger of this. The man had no mortal sins, but the priest urged him to go frequently nonetheless, suggesting that it could be pride that was keeping him away. He resolved then to start going regularly.

Although it is necessary to go to confession for mortal sins, it's important to go for venial sins also. Pope John Paul II taught:

> Though the Church knows and teaches that venial sins are forgiven in other ways too,…she does not cease to remind everyone of the special usefulness of the sacramental moment for these sins too. The frequent use of the Sacrament…strengthens the awareness that even minor sins offend God and harm the Church, the Body of Christ.[1]

When we confess venial sins, we develop a greater sensitivity to them and become more inclined to overcome them. Most people who commit mortal sins began with repeated venial sins and, thus weakened, fell into more serious sins.

We *need* confession to grow in our relationship with the Lord. Pius XII taught:

> [T]o ensure more rapid progress day by day in the path of virtue,

> We will that the pious practice of frequent confession…should be earnestly advocated. By it genuine self-knowledge is increased, Christian humility grows, bad habits are corrected, spiritual neglect and tepidity are resisted, the conscience is purified, the will strengthened, a salutary self-control is attained, and grace is increased in virtue of the Sacrament itself.[2]

We get a great deal of grace from this sacrament, and we grow in virtue as well. Saint Francis de Sales wrote,

> In confession you not only receive absolution from the…sins you confess, but also great strength to avoid them in the future, light to see them clearly, and abundant grace to repair whatever damage you have incurred. You will also practice the virtues of humility, obedience, simplicity, and charity. In the single act of confession you will exercise more virtues than in any other act whatsoever.[3]

Saint John Vianney said, "When you go to confession, you must understand…you are about to un-nail Our Lord."[4]

Pope John Paul II went to confession weekly, as did Saint Dominic Savio. Saints Thomas Aquinas, Margaret of Cortona and Bridget of Sweden went to confession just about every day. For anyone who is not prevented from going by external circumstances, frequent confession—at least once a month—is an essential part of holiness.

Knowledge of Sins

Whenever we meditate on the first luminous mystery, we should ask for the grace to know all our sins, as did the people who came for John's baptism in the Jordan. And we should ask that God reveal our sins gradually, so we will not be devastated by seeing them all at once.

We will surely never become holy if we don't develop a healthy sense of the horror of sin and a deep sense of sorrow for our sins. The abbot Dorotheus, in the early years of the Church, said, "It does not matter how many virtues a man may have, even if they are beyond number and limit. If he has turned from the path of self-accusation, he will never find peace."[5]

Earlier I mentioned a way to stay focused on overcoming sin: Make a list of your three worst sins and examine it every night before retiring. It could be fewer than three but never more, since it is hard to focus on more than three sins at a time, and sharp focus is what we need to truly reform. By seeing this small list each night on paper, you will develop a deeper awareness of your faults and will be more ready to correct them.

One of the goals of doing this is to come to a point where you can delete one of the items on the list and replace it with a lesser sin. And certainly one of the benefits of this is that, with these three things in mind, it is usually very easy to examine your conscience in preparation for confession.

The closer we get to God, the more we realize how far we are from him. This is because, as Saint John of the Cross wrote, when very bright sunlight shines in our room, we are able to see all the particles of dust in the air. So it is with intimacy with God: the closer we get to him, the more clearly we see our sins, and the more we want them wiped clean.

God in His mercy wants to wipe them clean! Let's take advantage of the wonderful sacrament of penance.

. . . . .

CHAPTER TWELVE

The Mass, "Source and Summit of the Christian Life"

The sacrifice of Christ and the sacrifice of the Eucharist are one single sacrifice: "The victim is one and the same: the same now offers through the ministry of priests, who then offered himself on the cross; only the manner of offering is different.... [I]n this divine sacrifice which is celebrated in the Mass, the same Christ who offered himself once in a bloody manner on the altar of the cross is contained and offered in an unbloody manner" (CCC, #1367, quoting the Council of Trent [1562]: *Doctrina de ss. Missae sacrificio,* c.2:DS 1743; cf. *Heb* 9:14, 27.)

Pope John Paul II taught, "The Eucharist is above all else a sacrifice."[1] And it is more: "The Mass is at the same time, and inseparably, the sacrificial memorial in which the sacrifice of the cross is perpetuated and the sacred banquet of communion with the Lord's body and blood" (CCC, #1382).

So the Mass is above all the re-presentation of the one sacrifice of Jesus' death on the cross. And it is also a sacred banquet of communion with our Eucharistic Lord. It is the fulfillment of all the Old Testament sacrifices: "[The Mass] is, finally, that [sacrifice] which was prefigured by various types of sacrifices during the period of nature and of the law [Genesis 4:4; 12:8 and elsewhere], which, namely, comprises all the good things signified by them, as being the consummation and perfection of them all."[2]

That means that all the Old Testament sacrifices—the sacrificial lambs, the bulls, the goats and the scapegoat in particular—were all foreshadowings of the true sacrifice of Jesus Christ on the cross. Those sacrifices had no power in themselves to remit sins, but insofar as they were related to the true sacrifice of Jesus, they had that power.

The Real Presence

Of course, for the Mass to truly be the reoffering of the sacrifice of Jesus' death on Calvary, He would have to be truly present in the eucharistic species. And He is. Jesus said:

> Truly, truly, I say to you, unless you eat the flesh of the Son of man and drink his blood, you have no life in you; he who eats my flesh and drinks my blood has eternal life, and I will raise him up at the last day. For my flesh is food indeed, and my blood is drink indeed. He who eats my flesh and drinks my blood abides in me, and I in him (John 6:53–56).

Right from the first century, the Church has taken these words literally, that the substance of bread and wine is changed miraculously into the substance of Jesus' Body and Blood. The "accidents"—the appearance, taste, shape and so on—remain those of bread and wine, but the substance (that is, what it is) is different.

When certain Protestants doubted the real presence of Christ in the Eucharist in the sixteenth century, the Council of Trent made clear the Church's position: "If anyone denies that in the sacrament of the most Holy Eucharist are contained truly, really and substantially the body and blood together with the soul and divinity of our Lord Jesus Christ, and consequently the whole Christ, but says that He is in it only as in a sign, or figure or force, let him be anathema."[3]

There have been a good number of miracles over the centuries that have confirmed the real presence of Jesus in the Eucharist. One involved a monk in Lanciano, Italy, in the eighth century, who doubted the real presence as he said Mass one day. Then, just after the consecration, he noticed that the host had been transformed into a circle of flesh, and the wine was changed into visible blood. As he began to weep with joy, he announced to the congregation: "O fortunate witnesses, to whom the Blessed God, to confound my unbelief, has wished to reveal Himself visible to our eyes! Come, brethren, and marvel at our God, so close to us. Behold the flesh and blood of our Most Beloved Christ."[4]

The congregation quickly came forward to see the miracle, and after Mass they went out to spread the news. Over the centuries many scientific tests have been made on these elements. In one such investigation it was discovered that the flesh was muscle tissue from the myocardium—that is, the wall of the heart— and contained no trace of a preservative. The flesh and the blood were of human origin, with the blood matching the blood type in the flesh. These miraculous relics can still be seen in the Church of St. Francis in Lanciano.[5]

There have been over thirty such miracles, reassurances from God that the Eucharist is truly the Body and Blood of Christ.

Sacred Banquet
The Mass is secondarily a "sacred banquet," and as such was prefigured by several sacred meals:

- the life-saving meal offered as hospitality to one who was encountered in the desert by nomads
- the joyful feast celebrating the covenant renewal with God

- the Passover meal celebrating the Jews' "passing over" from their slavery in Egypt to the Promised Land and God's "passing over" the Israelites when he struck down all the firstborn of the Egyptians
- the Feast of the Unleavened Bread, when the Jews celebrated new beginnings at the time of the wheat harvest in the spring, eating only unleavened bread for a week

What a rich background the Mass has!

In the Mass we celebrate our passing over from the slavery of sin and death to the new life of the final Promised Land, God's kingdom of grace and love. This passing over was made possible by the saving event of Christ's death on the cross. In the Mass we offer the Lamb of God, Jesus, and then partake in this eucharistic feast as a sign of our covenant renewal with the Lord. This new covenant is Christ and his law of love.

"From the liturgy, therefore, and especially from the eucharist, as from a font, grace is poured forth upon us; and the sanctification of men in Christ and the glorification of God, to which all other activities of the Church are directed as toward their end, is achieved in the most efficacious possible way."[6] In other words, nothing we might do, no prayer we might offer, could ever equal the superabundant power of the Mass.

Saint Bernard of Clairvaux wrote, "One merits more by devoutly assisting at a Holy Mass than by distributing all of his goods to the poor and traveling all over the world on pilgrimage."[7] Saint Francis de Sales wrote:

[T]he Sun of all spiritual exercises...[is] the most holy, sacred and Sovereign Sacrifice and Sacrament of the Eucharist—the very centre point of our Christian religion, the heart of all devotion, the soul of piety—that Ineffable Mystery which embraces the whole depth of Divine Love, by which God, giving Himself really to us, conveys all His Graces and favors to men with royal magnificence.

Prayer made in union with this Divine Sacrifice has untold power.[8]

The Council of Trent taught that the best way to aid the souls in purgatory is through the "sacrifice of the altar,"[9] that is, the Mass. This, of course, is why Catholics have for centuries had Masses said for their beloved dead. And Saint John Vianney said, "All good works taken together cannot have the value of one Holy Mass, because they are the works of men, whereas the Holy Mass is the work of God."[10]

Sunday Mass

Every Catholic has an obligation to attend Mass at least every Sunday. In light of all God has done for us, the least we can do is spend one hour every Sunday giving thanks to Him (*Eucharist* means "thanksgiving"). This is why the Church teaches, "On Sundays and other holy days of obligation the faithful are bound to participate in the Mass" (*CCC*, #2180, quoting *CIC*, canon 1247).

The Sunday Eucharist is the foundation and confirmation of all Christian practice. "For this reason the faithful are obliged to participate in the Eucharist on Sundays and other holy days of obligation unless excused for a serious reason (for example, illness, the care of infants) or dispensed by their own pastor. Those who deliberately fail in this obligation commit a grave sin" (*CCC*, #2181, cf. *CIC*, canon 1245). This obligation, of course, stems from the third commandment.

Notice that shopping, playing golf or soccer or tennis and going to a party are not mentioned as reasons to miss Sunday Mass. If we can't get to Mass on Sunday morning, we should get there Saturday evening or Sunday evening.

With the Internet and masstimes.org (a Web site that gives the Mass times at the ten closest churches for a given address or zip code), just about everyone should be able to find a Mass to fulfill the Sunday obligation, even when traveling. I know a layman who traveled through England (hardly a Catholic country) for a week and was able to attend Mass not only on Sunday but every day!

Certainly when we're sick or find ourselves unavoidably far from a church, we are excused. However, some seem to have many excuses for missing Sunday Mass, and others rarely need an excuse. This is a matter of priorities.

For those who are on the edge regarding Sunday Mass, this is not a question of holiness but of fulfilling the minimum obligation of love. The person who attends Sunday Mass and says a few prayers each night is barely living the faith and will find it difficult to avoid losing his faith in our secular world. Living the faith halfway is not living the gospel, and it won't satisfy the Christian heart.

A consideration that has been all but lost is the third commandment, which tells us to keep holy the Lord's Day. How few Christians make any effort to avoid working on Sunday so they can worship God and rest for His sake. The *Catechism* teaches: "On Sundays and other holy days of obligation, the faithful are to refrain from engaging in work or activities that hinder the worship owed to God, the joy proper to the Lord's Day, the performance of the works of mercy, and the appropriate relaxation of mind and body" (CCC, #2185, cf. CIC, canon 1247). And Pope John Paul II wrote, "In honouring God's 'rest,' man fully discovers himself, and thus the Lord's Day bears the profound imprint of God's blessing [see Genesis 2:3]."[11]

One young man in our parish worked seven days a week because he felt he needed to in order to support his family. At one point he decided to step out in faith and stop working Sundays. His income increased considerably, and he made more money in six days than he had in seven. God is ready to help us if we are willing to trust Him.

Daily Mass

If we receive so much grace from the Mass, and we must become so very holy to be ready to enter the kingdom, would it not be wise to consider daily Mass? Saint Francis de Sales wrote: "Strive then to your utmost to be present every day at this holy Celebration, in order that with the priest you may offer the Sacrifice of your Redeemer on behalf of yourself and the whole Church to God the Father."[12]

Whenever people come to me for spiritual direction, I ask them if they attend daily Mass. If not I encourage them either to start or, if they cannot, at least to pray that God will arrange things so that they can go. It seems that if they want help steering the ship, they should acquire the fuel themselves. In just about every case, those who have prayed for the grace of getting to daily Mass have been given it within a year.

There are many ways to get into the habit of daily Mass. I prayed for years about it before receiving the grace to attend. One day I committed to go for three months, and if that worked out, I would continue for life. It did. I know someone who went to one Mass during the week for a year, then two the next year and so forth. In six years he became a daily communicant.

What we should remember is that we should never tell God we can't go but rather ask Him to show us how we can. It seems that this is very much the sort of prayer God wants to answer!

Those who know the crucial importance of remaining in the state of grace, in God's love, will make great sacrifices to get to Mass every Sunday. But those who know the infinite value of the Mass, the superabundant grace it gives, will make great sacrifices to get to Mass every day.

. . . . .

CHAPTER THIRTEEN

Eucharistic Adoration

When I was in the seminary, I began to notice a woman who came often to pray in our chapel. I asked one of my classmates who she was, and he told me, "That's Peggy. She's been making a holy hour every day for nineteen years."

"Does she have any children?" I asked.

"I think she has six." He was right.

I stopped to speak to Peggy one day and asked how she had managed to make a regular holy hour with six children. She told me she had arranged for baby-sitters or traded child care times with her sisters. She would go to convents and ask to use their chapel when the churches were closed, or she would come to our seminary, since our chapel was always open.

I asked her to write me a couple pages on her experience, so I could share her story with others when I was ordained. She agreed to do so. I had to remind her a couple of times, but finally she came up with six pages of her beautiful story.

One Woman's Nineteen-Year Holy Hour

Peggy first heard about holy hours in Catholic high school, where the students made one weekly. Even though she went to Mass daily, she was a rebel, playing hooky eighty-five times before the school caught her. She did everything she could to avoid doing her chores at home, and her sisters hated her for that.

When Peggy went off to college, she began to make a holy hour each day because she was so homesick. But once she got over being homesick, she tapered off the holy hours.

She married at age twenty-two and had four children in succession. She was still undisciplined and had no interest in housework, though her husband wanted everything neat and clean.

Peggy was subject to wild mood changes, going from high to low and back again every few days. Alas, she overdid during the highs and wore herself out, bringing on another low. Her husband worked long hours, so she felt all alone trying to raise her four children.

When she had a miscarriage, she became so upset that she tried to kill herself, though she was still attending daily Mass and spending a half hour or more in prayer each day. Her husband was so angry with her at this point that he refused to come to the hospital.

Because her husband was a morning person and she was not, they'd have some sort of fight just about every morning. She loved her children and wanted the marriage to succeed, but she was overwhelmed. She saw no way to solve their huge personality problems.

Finally Peggy realized she would have to do something dramatic to turn her life around. She decided to get up each day at 4:45 AM, an hour before her husband. Not surprisingly, it was very hard at first, but she began to take delight in this early morning time. When she heard Bishop Sheen speak of the eucharistic holy hour, she decided that's what she needed and made a commitment to do it every day.

The changes came quickly. Her moods became more even; she came to appreciate her husband, her children and even the house she had to clean and the clothes she had to launder. By the grace of the holy hour, she learned to stay calm when her husband lost his temper, instead of yelling back at him. In time his bad temper calmed down.

Peggy's laziness was changed into vigor, her resentment into grateful acceptance. She found true peace for the first time and came to see Jesus as her first love and constant helper. When her children became involved with drugs, she brought them in spirit to the holy hour and entrusted their lives to Jesus. She was confident He would straighten them out, and He did. One even became a daily communicant.

Peace began to reign in their home, and she and her husband learned to love each other deeply. She gave up on controlling her life and others and just entrusted all to her Eucharistic Love. Even in the midst of trials and sufferings, she was able to keep her peace and serenity. She found her strength each day in the Eucharist.

By God's grace Peggy was able to start a pregnancy aid group and a women's prayer group. The prayer group began with just a few women, and in seven years it grew to a hundred. Many of the women were near divorce when they came, and their families were in shambles. About twenty of them were making a daily holy hour, and many more made a weekly one. Through this prayer their marriages turned around, and harmony came to their homes.

Peggy's closing words were: "Our Lord is a precious, wonderful, loving redeemer. He longs to touch and heal each of us in His love. He longs to give us His light and life, if only we come and let Him refresh us. I pray that you will be a holy priest, madly in love with Jesus Christ, and that you will come to know His wonderful, gentle love in the Eucharist. May you never lose sight of Him and His love."

One might ask, if the Mass is "the source and summit of the Christian life" (*Lumen Gentium*, 11), how much more could the holy hour have added to this woman's already admirable practice of daily Mass? Simply this: The deeper one's prayer life, the more perfectly a person is able to participate in the Mass; thus the more grace they are able to receive from the Mass itself. The more Peggy prayed, the more grace she received from the Mass.

And grace she received—in abundance. What a gift she has given us in sharing that grace!

Bishop Sheen

Bishop Fulton J. Sheen is the person who seems to have popularized the eucharistic holy hour in this country. He was asked shortly before he died in 1979 what had inspired him to take up this practice. His answer was surprising. He said it was a young Chinese girl, age eleven.

When the Communists took power in China, they made a certain priest a prisoner in his own house. He was able to see the church from his window. He saw the Communists break open the tabernacle and throw a ciborium down, with all the hosts spilling out on the floor. The priest had counted the hosts; there were thirty-two.

A little girl had seen this as she prayed in the back of the church. That night, and for thirty-one more nights, she came back, snuck by the guards and prayed before the hosts for an hour to make reparation for the terrible desecration of the Eucharist. Each night at the end of the hour, she would lean down and receive a host with her tongue, since at that time a layperson could not take the host in the hand.

On the last night, when she had received the last host, one of the guards saw her leave. He followed her and beat her to death. The priest watched this in horror.

When Fulton Sheen heard this story, he was so moved that he resolved to spend one hour each day of his priesthood before the Blessed Sacrament. And of course, by his talks given all over the world, he inspired many others, especially priests—including this one—to do the same. It was one of his talks on the holy hour that inspired Peggy to make her daily holy hour.[1]

As Bishop Sheen pointed out, the holy hour is one of the few direct requests our blessed Lord made of His apostles: "[C]ould you not watch with me one hour?" (Matthew 26:40). It is my hope that the example of that little Chinese girl, of Bishop Sheen and of Peggy will inspire many reading this to do the same: Spend an hour in adoration of our Eucharistic Lord each day.

It is wonderful that many parishes have begun to have perpetual adoration of the Blessed Sacrament, exposed in the monstrance, over the past twenty-five years. However, most eucharistic holy hours, including those of the saints, Bishop Sheen and Peggy, have been made not before the monstrance but before the tabernacle. Although it is a great privilege to pray before the monstrance, praying before the tabernacle is also a great privilege, and we should take advantage of this when exposition is not available.

Some may ask, "What would I do during an hour of prayer?" Well, here are some possibilities: Meditate on Sacred Scripture, especially the readings for the next day's Mass; meditate on the mysteries of the rosary; make the Stations of the Cross; pray the Liturgy of the Hours. Or you might just do as a parishioner of Saint John Vianney did during his many hours before the Blessed Sacrament: "I look at the good Lord, and he looks at me."[2]

Why should you pray before the Blessed Sacrament as opposed to some other place? If the examples of Peggy and

Bishop Sheen aren't enough, the saints should inspire us. Saint Francis of Assisi, it seems, was the first to go and pray in churches where the Blessed Sacrament was reserved for the sick. Saint Clare spent long hours in prayer before the Blessed Sacrament, and her face would glow when she came out. Saint John of the Cross slept only two or three hours a night because he found his rest praying before the Blessed Sacrament. His face too shone with brightness at times.

Pope John Paul II is said to have spent two hours a day before the Blessed Sacrament in prayer; and Blessed Mother Teresa of Calcutta and her nuns spent three hours a day there. What better way to do as Our Lord has asked, "Come to Me, all you who are weary and find life burdensome and I will refresh you" (see Matthew 11:28).

He will indeed refresh us!

. . . . .

Loving

Our

Neighbor

CHAPTER FOURTEEN

The Spiritual Works of Mercy

Loving our neighbor as ourselves is the second essential law of love for the Christian. It might seem obvious to us just what we should do to love others, but the Church actually presents us with a list: the spiritual and corporal works of mercy.

In this chapter we'll discuss the seven spiritual works of mercy:

1. Instructing the ignorant
2. Counseling the doubtful
3. Admonishing the sinner
4. Bearing wrongs patiently
5. Forgiving all injuries
6. Comforting the afflicted
7. Praying for the living and the dead

Instructing and Counseling

The first spiritual work of mercy, instructing people about the faith, is an extremely important one. It was fashionable in the latter part of the twentieth century for religious to give up teaching and go out to help the poor. Helping the poor is a good thing, but these people were forgoing a spiritual work of mercy for a corporal. Thomas Aquinas pointed out that the spiritual works are more beneficial than the corporal.[1]

The primary teachers of children about the faith—and everything, for that matter—are their parents. So parents should be very concerned for their children's education, both at home and in school. Saint Augustine allegedly said that the best three ways to teach children the faith were, first, by example; second, by example; and third, by example. Every parent is a teacher simply by what he or she does, and children seem to observe very well. It is hard to overestimate the influence parents have on their children and how important their teaching is.

Teachers in schools, and especially in religion classes, should be skilled at teaching. They must avoid the two great sins of teaching, especially if they teach religion. The worst sin, of course, is to teach something other than the truth. The second-worst sin is to make the subject matter boring.

A religion teacher should do everything possible to make religion interesting. One thing that keeps interest up is to teach the students about heaven, hell and purgatory in the first few classes and then relate everything else to their salvation. There is something very interesting about one's eternal destiny. Of course, telling stories, using the Socratic method of asking questions and having little contests in class can help as well.

Part of instructing the ignorant is evangelizing. Christians have an obligation to spread the faith in whatever way they can. Pope Paul VI wrote, "[I]t is unthinkable that a person should accept the Word and give himself to the kingdom without becoming a person who bears witness to it and proclaims it in his turn."[2] Pope John Paul II wrote, "Those who are incorporated in the Catholic Church ought to sense their privilege and for that very reason their greater obligation of bearing witness to the faith and to the Christian life as a service to their brothers and sisters and as a fitting response to God."[3] Each believer has the duty to pass on the faith by word, example, writing or any other means available.

One woman did her part by giving prayer cards to fellow patients while she was in the hospital. Saint Maximilian Kolbe would give out miraculous medals to just about everyone he met. Whatever our method, we need to spread our most precious gift, our faith.

The second spiritual work of mercy is to counsel those who doubt the faith. It is similar to the first, but rather than providing information that is not already known, it means shoring up belief in a doctrine that is known but doubted. So, for example, Harry can counsel a doubtful George by explaining to him why God permits suffering in the world.

Admonishing and Praying

Admonishing, that is, warning, the sinner is another spiritual work, one that takes some skill. You must be gentle yet firm enough to make the person aware that he or she is headed for disaster. For example, if Mrs. Jones tells her twenty-five-year-old son Melvin six times a day that he is going to hell because he moved in with his girlfriend, Melvin will probably tune her out. But if she reminds him lovingly but solemnly, at certain key times, that she is praying for his salvation, that might well bring about a conversion.

Of course, in conjunction with any warning of sinners must come the spiritual work of praying for them. No real Christian could ever doubt the value of praying for another. Carlo Carretto, a devout Catholic author who spent ten years praying in the desert, wrote, "I am completely convinced that one never wastes one's time by praying; there is no more helpful way of helping those we love."[4]

Bishop Sheen once noted that the paralytic of Capernaum was healed because of the prayers and efforts of the four men who let him down through the roof. And he had his sins forgiven as well!

I knew a woman who prayed twenty-five years for her father to return to the faith. He was reconciled to God on his deathbed. We should never lose heart in praying for those for whom we care.

When Mary appeared in August 1917 to the three little seers at Fatima, she told them, "Pray, pray a great deal, and make sacrifices for sinners, for many souls go to hell because they have no one to sacrifice and pray for them."[5] In other words, our prayers and sacrifices can actually bring people who are heading for eternal ruin the grace to convert and be saved.

Prayer for others is included in every Sunday Mass and in both Morning and Evening Prayer in the Liturgy of the Hours. Saint Paul wrote, "First of all, then, I urge that supplications, prayers, intercessions, and thanksgivings be made for all men, for kings and all who are in high positions, that we may lead a quiet and peaceable life, godly and respectful in every way" (1 Timothy 2:1–2). Jesus tells us to pray for our persecutors (see Matthew 5:44), and he prayed for Peter that his faith would not fail (see Luke 22:31). And Paul often asked the faithful to pray for him and promised his prayers for them.

Saint Thérèse of Lisieux felt moved to pray for souls, especially great sinners. A murderer named Pranzini was about to be executed for some brutal killings. She prayed hard, offering the infinite merits of Christ for his conversion. She also got her sister to pray for him and to have a Mass offered for him.

Thérèse looked in the newspaper the day after Pranzini's execution. She learned that he had refused to go to confession, but when he got to the scaffold, he grabbed the accompanying priest's crucifix and kissed the wounds three times. Thérèse's prayers were answered.[6]

And how helpful it is to pray for the *dead*! In one parish the retired pastor would always "canonize" the deceased when he said a funeral Mass, implicitly discouraging family and friends from praying for the person. All the other priests in the rectory told him not to come anywhere near their funeral. They wanted people to pray and pray and pray for them when they died!

Saint Ambrose wrote, "Everything which we offer God out of charity for the departed is changed into merit for us, and after death we will find the hundredfold."[7] Saint Gertrude offered all she could for the souls in purgatory, and at death the Lord appeared to her and told her that for her efforts for these souls, "I will remit...all the pains which you were to have suffered. Moreover, as I have promised a hundredfold to those who enkindle My love, I wish to reward you further by increasing the degree of glory which awaits you above.... [A]ll the souls whom you have aided will come to lead you into [heaven] amid great rejoicing."[8]

What is the greatest prayer we can offer for the holy souls? The Mass, as the Council of Trent declared. Both Saint Jerome and Saint Augustine taught that the holy souls feel no pain during a Mass at which they are prayed for.[9]

Indulgences

Another powerful thing we can do for the holy souls is to offer indulgences for them. Alas, this practice was much abused in the sixteenth century. Its validity was reiterated as a dogma at the Council of Trent. The scriptural basis for indulgences was given as Matthew 16:19 and John 20:23.[10]

A plenary indulgence eliminates all temporal punishment due to sin. In other words, it removes the need for purgatory. A partial indulgence eliminates some of the temporal punishment. We may apply an indulgence to ourselves or to a soul in purgatory, but not to another living person.

To gain a plenary indulgence, a number of conditions must be met:

1. An indulgenced act, such as praying the rosary in a public oratory, a family, religious community or other group; reading or hearing Sacred Scripture; adoring the Blessed Sacrament for at least half an hour or piously praying the Way of the Cross.[11]

2. Sacramental confession within twenty[12] days before or after the day the indulgence is sought. One confession can satisfy for a good number of plenary indulgences.

3. Eucharistic Communion on the same day as the indulgenced act.

4. Prayer for the Holy Father (One Our Father and one Hail Mary suffice, but other prayers may be used.)

5. Detachment from all sin, including venial sin. This does not mean freedom from all sin but from attachment to sin: In effect, you have no affection for the sin and are sincerely trying to stop committing it.[13]

To explain attachment to sin, let's say someone is habitually irritable in the morning. If the person is sincerely trying to overcome this, then he is detached. If, however, the person has no intention of reforming, then he would not be a candidate for a plenary indulgence. From this it should be clear that the person seeking a plenary indulgence should be trying for the perfection

A CATHOLIC'S GUIDE TO THE SPIRITUAL LIFE

of which Jesus spoke: "You, therefore, must be perfect, as your heavenly Father is perfect" (Matthew 5:48).

If a plenary indulgence is not obtained because of attachment to a venial sin, the indulgence would still be partial. You may ordinarily receive one plenary indulgence per day but any number of partial indulgences.

It should be noted that if all the conditions are met for a plenary indulgence, the indulgence does indeed wipe out all *our* temporal punishment due to sin if offered for ourselves, but it does not necessarily do so for the dead person for whom we might offer it. Indulgences for the dead are offered by "suffrage," that is, as a prayer, without certainty that it is plenary. The effects of such an indulgence are "according to the hidden designs of God's mercy."[14] Nonetheless, such an indulgence would be a powerful aid to a person in purgatory.

When a sister in her convent died, Saint Mary Magdalene de Pazzi and the other sisters offered all the indulgences they had received that day for her soul. That same day the saint observed the recently dead sister's soul ascending to heaven as she prayed for her, and Jesus appeared to Saint Mary to tell her that it was due to the indulgences that the sister had so quickly been freed from the pains of purgatory.[15]

Happy the person who receives Communion at Mass daily and prays the rosary before or after and daily fulfills all the conditions for a plenary indulgence for the holy souls in purgatory. Happy, too, the person who offers many partial indulgences daily for the holy souls. What an army of people he will have praying for him and greeting him thankfully when he gets to heaven!

With all their power, indulgences are not as beneficial as the Mass: "In accordance with tradition, participation in the Sacrifice of the Mass or the Sacraments is not enriched by indulgences, by reason of the surpassing efficacy for 'sanctification and purification' that they have in themselves."[16]

How important it is that we never forget to pray for the dead!

Other Spiritual Works

Comforting the sorrowing is another spiritual work, one that especially comes into play with the death of a friend's loved one but could apply to any misfortune. Just being present for a friend who is hurting can be a great gift.

One of the most difficult spiritual works is forgiving injuries. Those who spend more time contemplating their own wounds than the wounds of Christ will always have trouble forgiving. Perhaps that is why the saints spent such long hours meditating on Christ's sufferings.

To forgive your enemy means ultimately to pray for him or her. Not to forgive is to place your feelings above his salvation.

As we mentioned earlier, forgiving is not optional. Jesus said that if we want God to forgive us, we must forgive others. Anyone who has found the kingdom of God, that "pearl of great price" Jesus spoke of, would hardly let an unforgiven injury stand in his way of possessing it, would he? If a person will not forgive, perhaps he has not yet found that "pearl" in his heart.

Bearing injustices patiently also goes against our grain as human beings. Justice is a virtue, but bearing injustices for the sake of Christ is a greater virtue, because in doing so we exercise the virtue of loving God more than our own feelings. We think not of the world's justice but of God's. Many a wise man has said that there is no justice in this world. Those who cling to their own justice in this life may well lose hold of the kingdom of God.

Once Dominic Savio was blamed for a prank that another boy had played on a teacher. Dominic said nothing and took the punishment, which was to kneel in the middle of the room for a long time. Before long the other boys told the teacher that Dominic hadn't done it. When the teacher asked Dominic why he had taken the blame, he replied, "Because that boy had been in trouble before and would have been expelled.... Besides, I remembered that our Lord had once been falsely accused, too."[17]

. . . . .

CHAPTER FIFTEEN

The Corporal Works of Mercy

The corporal works of mercy are also seven:

1. Feeding the hungry
2. Giving drink to the thirsty
3. Clothing the naked
4. Sheltering the homeless
5. Visiting the sick
6. Visiting the imprisoned
7. Burying the dead

Most of these come from Matthew 25:31–46 ("I was hungry and you gave me food...."), with the addition of burying the dead, which is based on Tobit 12. And "I was a stranger and you welcomed me" (Matthew 25:35) is interpreted to mean sheltering the homeless.

Caring for the Poor

The first four corporal works of mercy can be combined into one: helping the poor. Each one of us has an *obligation* to help the poor, as Jesus taught in the parable of the sheep and the goats (Matthew 25:31–46). In fact, he said that when we help them we help *Him!*

The First Letter of John adds to this: "But if any one has the world's goods and sees his brother in need, yet closes his heart against him, how does God's love abide in him? Little children, let us not love in word or speech but in deed and in truth" (1 John 3:17–18).

So we have an obligation to help the poor, but how much? The answer is broadly given in Scripture. In the Old Testament it is recommended that we give one-tenth of our income back to the Lord (Deuteronomy 14:28–29; Numbers 18:23–24). Some suggest that we give 5 percent to the poor and 5 percent to the Church.

Some people, at least for a time, might struggle to give even 5 percent. Others may find that they can live quite comfortably giving 20 or 25 percent. How can you be morally certain that you are giving enough?

It seems you should feel you have made a sacrifice. Pope John Paul II said in 1979, "You must never be content to leave [the poor] just the crumbs from the feast. You must take of your substance, and not just of your abundance, in order to help them. And you must treat them like guests at your family table."[1]

All the saints were deeply generous. The woman who anointed Jesus with expensive perfumed oil did not pour it out drop by drop but broke the jar, thereby insuring that she had to pour it *all* on Jesus (Mark 14:3). We should pray for such generosity, giving to the Lord and His people without counting the cost.

Saint Ignatius of Loyola wrote this Prayer for Generosity:

Lord, teach me to be generous.
Teach me to serve you as you deserve;
to give and not to count the cost,
to fight and not to heed the wounds,
to toil and not to seek for rest,

> to labor and not to ask for reward,
> save that of knowing that I do your will.[2]

Should you give to every charity that sends an appeal through the mail? No, probably not. If you do you may have to write hundreds of checks a year. Better to choose a few good charities and ignore the others.

There is another group of the "poor" who are often overlooked: unborn children. Pope John Paul II wrote, "To this list [in Matthew 25] also we could add other ways of acting, in which Jesus is present in each case as the *one who has been rejected*. In this way he would identify with…the child conceived and then rejected 'You did not welcome me'!"[3]

It is not enough to be theoretically pro-life to avoid God's wrath; we must act decisively to help protect the most rejected human beings in the Western world, children in the womb. We must surely vote pro-life and contribute to pro-life organizations (these would be fundamental). We should also help women in crisis pregnancies and be passionate in our efforts to help the world see the huge social injustice of abortion in every way we can. We must not rest until these children are again protected by law. No Christian is excused from this moral battle.

Social Justice

Helping the poor involves not just our individual efforts but our commitment as a nation. Supporting humane working conditions, just trade agreements and justice for immigrants are just some of the things the Church has urged us to be involved with. Various popes have issued a number of social encyclicals, and we should be aware of the teaching therein so as to understand our obligations toward the poor in the political sphere. Here I name a few of these encyclicals, with a brief summary of their key points:

Rerum Novarum (1891, Leo XIII) stated that workers are to be treated not as slaves but as persons worthy of a decent wage, so that their lives may reflect human dignity.

Quadrigesimo Anno (1931, Pius XI) criticized socialism and unrestrained capitalism and called for a more just distribution of goods by the rich.

Mater et Magistra (1961, John XXIII) called for all citizens to receive benefits from economic growth, and workers some share in a company's profits. Rich nations must be concerned for poor nations and help them without manipulating them.

Centesimus Annus (1991, John Paul II) condemned socialism because it reduces the person to a mere cog in the economic system. The pope praised elements of capitalism (free markets, "private property and the resulting responsibility for the means of production, as well as free human creativity in the economic sector"[4]) but noted its flaw if it does not promote integral human freedom.

It is, of course, impossible to cover these and other social justice encyclicals in just a few words, but I hope that this list will provide a taste of the Church's global concern for the poor.

Of particular concern today is the issue of immigrants. We should remember the words of Jesus in Matthew 25:35, "I was a stranger and you welcomed me." It seems that the Christian way to handle immigration is not to deport all those who are here illegally but to work toward a fair procedure to help them become legal immigrants. We should also promote enforceable laws that make it easier for immigrants to enter our country.

The Church taught in 2004: "Christians must in fact promote an authentic *culture of welcome*...capable of accepting the truly human values of the immigrants over and above any difficulties caused by living together with persons who are different.... Christians will accomplish all this by means of a truly fraternal welcome in the sense of St Paul's admonition, 'Welcome one another then, as Christ welcomed you, for the glory of God' (Rm 15:7)."[5]

Caring for the Sick

Catherine of Siena visited hospitals, which back in her time were dirty, disease-ridden places. She always volunteered to care for those with the most repulsive diseases. One such patient was a woman with an ugly case of breast cancer. Because of her stinking disease and dirty bed, hardly anyone came to take care of her. Catherine would wait on this woman hand and foot and showed her nothing but kindness, much to the woman's surprise.

But instead of being grateful to Catherine for her loving care, the woman showed her hatred, spreading rumors that Catherine had sinned against purity. Catherine ignored it all and continued to serve this cranky woman. Catherine's mother became angry over the rumors and told her to stay away from the woman. Catherine listened respectfully, then knelt at her mother's feet and reminded her of all the agony Jesus endured for us and the hatred He received in return. She asked if her mother wanted her to let the poor woman suffer a miserable death without a single friend. Her mother changed her mind and praised Catherine for her goodness.

Catherine prayed and prayed for the woman and continued to serve her. At one point the poor woman saw Catherine clothed with light, which shone upon her and her bed and relieved her suffering. After this she recognized Catherine's goodness and repented of her bad treatment of her. She asked Catherine to forgive her and began to tell others of Catherine's kindness and to correct the shameful lies she had spread. [6]

Jesus made it clear in Matthew 25 that visiting the sick is something we must do if we hope to enter the kingdom. Just about all the saints were eager to visit the sick. Saint Camillus de Lellis saw Christ in every sick person; he even asked them to forgive his sins. He founded an order to serve the sick in hospitals at a time when the sick were treated like dirt.

A story is told of some young sisters who had just joined Mother Teresa's Missionaries of Charity. They came back from visiting the sick in a nearby hospital saying joyfully, "We have seen Jesus; we have talked to Him."

A reporter came to visit Mother Teresa and found her stooped over someone who had a repulsive disease. The reporter looked down on Mother Teresa washing this patient and said, "I wouldn't do that for a million dollars." Mother Teresa looked up and said, "Neither would I."[7]

There are two things I learned when working in a hospital one semester. First, you need not say much to patients. Whether you pray with them, just stay with them quietly or just listen, they are appreciative. The other thing is that it is better to make several short visits than one long one. There is a certain "creative absence" that actually makes it better to take time out to call family members or go somewhere for prayer or nourishment and then return. This is what I was taught, and experience seemed to bear it out.

One thing that delighted me in visiting people in nursing homes was how ready the residents were for a good laugh. We have a tendency to become saddened by the surroundings, aroma and conditions in nursing homes. But the Lord doesn't invite us there to be sad. We have the ability to bring a little joy to people in these situations, and they are often quick to respond. If we have a strong prayer life and have gone to the Lord in prayer before visiting a nursing home or hospital, we will have the power to overcome the sadness of the situation with God's joy. And in turn, the residents will often cheer *us* up!

Visiting the Imprisoned and the Bereaved

Most of us don't get many chances to visit the imprisoned. But if we do get such a chance, we should jump at it, knowing that it is Christ we visit. And it is much easier to visit prisons today than it was at the time of Blessed Margaret of Costello.

This little blind, hunchbacked girl used to visit the local prison with her third order Dominican group. The prisoners were chained day and night to the walls. There were no bathrooms, which led to a disgusting stench as well as a breeding ground for disease. Half the prisoners died yearly of "jail fever." Margaret and her Dominican friends would bring clean linens, food and the love of Christ to these poor souls.[8]

One unjustly imprisoned man would often curse God over his sad predicament. He was deeply moved when Margaret stood up and prayed quietly while her partner bathed his wounds. Margaret was lifted off the ground, and her ugliness was transformed into beauty. When she returned to the ground, the previously unresponsive prisoner whispered, "Little Margaret, please pray for me." He was a changed man from that point on.[9]

Although "burying the dead" could mean just that in some remote areas, for most of us it entails being present to those who have lost loved ones, especially at funerals and viewings. A funeral can be difficult for family and friends, and to see a familiar face is a great consolation. Burying the dead is a corporal work of mercy, but it touches on two spiritual works of mercy, comforting the sorrowing and praying for the living and the dead.

Sometimes we are quite ready to go out and serve others corporally or spiritually, but we fail to serve our own family members. Praying for brothers and sisters and parents, visiting them when they are sick and consoling them in their trials should be priorities for the Christian. Charity begins at home!

The Church gives us these lists of good works to help guide us in the way of loving our neighbor. We ought to reflect on these often and attempt to participate in them at every opportunity.

. . . . .

The Life

of

Virtue

CHAPTER SIXTEEN

The Theological Virtues: Faith, Hope and Charity

"[I]t is necessary that your foundation consist of more than prayer and contemplation. If you do not strive for the virtues and practice them, you will always be dwarfs."[1] So wrote Saint Teresa of Ávila.

Before considering the life of virtue, we might ask: What exactly is a virtue? Essentially it's a good habit regarding some activity; for example, love of God, kindness and justice are virtues.

Truly living a holy life is not primarily about keeping the Ten Commandments but about developing virtues. Obeying the Ten Commandments will keep you from sin, but developing all the virtues will make you holy.

Saint Paul speaks to us of virtue in his Letter to the Colossians:

> Put on then, as God's chosen ones, holy and beloved, compassion, kindness, lowliness, meekness, and patience, forbearing one another and, if one has a complaint against another, forgiving each other; as the Lord has forgiven you, so you also must forgive. And over all these put on love, which binds everything together in perfect harmony. (Colossians 3:12–14)

Faith, hope and charity (or love) are the theological virtues. We received them at baptism; we are free to act on them or not. Faith comes first, providing the object of our hope, and then follows love, love of the good we hope for, God. Love is the greatest of virtues. "So faith, hope, love abide, these three; but the greatest of these is love" (1 Corinthians 13:13).

Faith

"[F]aith is the assurance of things hoped for, the conviction of things not seen" (Hebrews 11:1). To believe or to have faith, as Saint Augustine taught, is to "think with assent."[2]

Faith should begin with believing in God. Then we believe what He tells us in Sacred Scripture. Finally, because we believe, we accept his Word as the rule of our life.

We don't start by examining everything God teaches and deciding if it's true. That could take forever! Faith is believing what we cannot see or understand. "Understanding," said Saint Augustine, "is the reward of faith. Therefore do not seek to understand in order to believe, but believe that you may understand."[3]

At the same time it makes sense to believe in God, especially from the order we find in the world. And we believe in Jesus as God because He convinced at least ten skeptics to die for the truth of His resurrection. We believe in all that Jesus taught because God doesn't err or lie. God actually gives us inspiration from the Holy Spirit to move us from unbelief to belief.

Can a person be holy if he or she rejects some Church teachings? No. For the saints, belief in Church teaching was a given. The 1983 *Code of Canon Law* states:

> A person must believe with divine and Catholic faith all those things contained in the word of God, written or handed on, that is, in the one deposit of faith entrusted to the Church, and at the same time proposed as divinely revealed either by the solemn magisterium of the Church or by its ordinary and universal magisterium which is manifested by the common adherence of the Christian faithful under the leadership of the sacred magisterium; therefore all are bound to avoid any doctrines whatsoever contrary to them.[4]

Of course, the necessity to believe all the Church teaches is itself a truth from God, given to us by Jesus when He said to His apostles, "He who hears you hears me, and he who rejects you rejects me, and he who rejects me rejects him who sent me" (Luke 10:16). The descendants of the apostles are the pope and bishops.

Now, this only applies to teachings that are proposed as divinely revealed, either by the solemn magisterium, that is, a solemn definition by the pope *ex cathedra*, or by the ordinary magisterium. What about teachings that are not considered divinely revealed? May a good Catholic ignore these?

No. In 1964 Vatican II taught that the faithful must always hold fast to the teachings of the pope:

> This religious submission of mind and will must be shown in a special way to the authentic magesterium of the Roman Pontiff, even when he is not speaking *ex cathedra*; that is, it must be shown in such a way that his supreme magesterium is acknowledged with reverence, the judgments made by him are sincerely adhered to, according to his manifest mind and will.[5]

So the faithful must conform their thinking to the doctrines of the Church. Although it would be seriously sinful to not accept a moral teaching of the Church—for example, the teaching on social justice or on masturbation—it would not be a sin against faith, nor would it be heresy. However, the fact that one had avoided heresy in denying such moral teachings would not be much of a consolation when standing before the Lord on Judgment Day.

Blessed Cardinal Newman gave an insight into the believing Christian in a hymn he wrote, which includes these words:

> And I hold in veneration,
> For the love of [Christ] alone,

Holy Church as his creation,
and her teachings as his own.[6]

What of those who have never heard about Jesus Christ or about God? Are they guilty of a sin against faith?

No. If a person is in blameless ignorance of God, he will be judged according to the law written in his heart to do good and avoid evil. By following this as best he can, he can be saved.

How do we grow in faith? By asking God often to increase our faith, as did the apostles (see Luke 17:5), and by seeking God's grace through prayer, sacraments and participating in the Mass.

Hope

At a party many years ago, I was discussing religion and God with a man perhaps in his sixties. At one point he said, "It is presumptuous to think anyone would go to heaven." The man was seriously lacking in the virtue of hope. I responded, "It would be presumptuous if Christ hadn't promised it."

Hope is the theological virtue by which we look forward with confidence to supernatural happiness with God. It is striving with a restless heart and patient expectation toward the future good of union with God in His kingdom. "The virtue of hope is preeminently the virtue of the *status viatoris* [condition of being a pilgrim or one on the way]," says Josef Pieper.[7]

Hope too we receive freely from God at baptism. If we act on this gift, we are said to "have hope."

Hope initially strives for the reward of heaven for the self, but as we deepen our love for God, we seek to be with God for His sake, because we are grateful, and we wish Him the happiness of possessing us in love, since that is why He created us. Nonetheless, the initial hoping for heaven for our sake is something good, as was taught by the Council of Trent.[8]

Our hope is based on the death and resurrection of Jesus. It is "through Him that we have become certain of God." And it is in prayer that our hope begins. Pope Benedict XVI taught, "A first essential setting for learning hope is prayer."[9]

There is another sort of hope, natural hope, which according to Joseph Pieper, "blossoms with the strength of youth and withers when youth withers." Pieper goes on to quote the *Summa* of Saint Thomas Aquinas: "For youth, the future is long and the past is short."[10]

Children often believe they will be professional athletes when they grow up. They'll be quite successful and rich, and of course, they'll never grow old. As people grow up they realize that many of the unrealistic dreams they had will not happen. This seems to be at the heart of the mid-life crisis, in which people ask, "Is that all there is?" The more people are concerned with this world rather than the next, the more unpleasant this crisis will be.

Supernatural hope, on the other hand, is a constant source of youthfulness, because it provides an eternal future. Thus it should be an excellent remedy for the mid-life crisis. Who can deny the youthfulness of Saint Teresa of Ávila or Saint John Bosco, even in their later years, or closer to our own time, the youthfulness of Blessed Mother Teresa of Calcutta?

Sins Against Hope

There are two sins against hope, despair and presumption. Despair kills hope by denying there is anything to hope for. One who despairs sees his own sins as unforgivable, greater than God's mercy. On the other hand, presumption kills hope by presuming salvation. One guilty of presumption convinces himself that he has somehow arrived at the state of salvation and is unable to go astray.

While we should have confidence that we will end up in God's kingdom if we live in His way, we should have a healthy fear of losing heaven while we still have freedom. The Council of Trent warned:

> Let no one promise oneself any security about this gift [of eternal life] with absolute certitude, although all should place their firmest hope in God's help. For, unless they themselves are unfaithful to his grace, God, who began the good work, will bring it to completion, effecting both the will and the execution. Yet, "let anyone who thinks he stands take heed not to fall" [1 Cor 10:12] and let one "work out one's salvation in fear and trembling" [Phil 2:12] in labours, in vigils, in almsgiving, in prayers and offerings, in fastings and chastity [cf. 2 Cor 6:3ff]. Knowing that they are reborn unto the hope of glory [cf.1 Pet 1:3] and not yet unto glory, they should be in dread about the battle they still have to wage with the flesh, the world and the devil....[11]

"There are two things that kill the soul," said Saint Augustine, "despair and false hope."[12] Both destroy our status as pilgrims on our way to God.[13]

The mercy of God is far greater than all sins put together. God the Father told Saint Faustina, "Encourage souls to place great trust in My fathomless mercy. Let the weak, sinful soul have no fear to approach Me, for even if it had more sins than there are grains of sand in the world, all would be drowned in the immeasurable depths of My mercy."[14]

Where does despair come from? It often comes from disordered sexual activity or lust, as Saint Thomas Aquinas taught, but more often from sloth. The love of sexual pleasures often causes a distaste for spiritual things by comparison. A person despairs of ever attaining spiritual wholeness again, thinking that he will never be able to detach himself from this exciting and stimulating activity. What he fails to realize is that after a time of painful withdrawal from lust, the spiritual life becomes sweet again.

Sloth, on the other hand, is a sadness over the divine good in mankind, over the fact that we are created in the image and likeness of God and that thus we can be great by God's grace. Rather than call on God for help, the slothful person gives up.

The terrible thing about despair is that there is not even an ounce of pleasure in it. God the Father said to Saint Catherine of Siena, "[T]here is no pleasure and nothing but intolerable suffering in [despair]. One who despairs despises My mercy, making his sin to be greater than mercy and goodness."[15]

Presumption is a far more prevalent sin against hope. It is the belief that one is assured of salvation. We should remember the words of Saint Paul quoted above, "[W]ork out your own salvation with fear and trembling" (Philippians 2:12).

Perhaps just as harmful as presumption is a limited or even negative image of heaven. A healthy idea of heaven, as I have mentioned before, is a wonderful incentive to struggle, to allow the Lord to transform us and make us new creations in Christ. And a concept that will keep us from being selfish in our hope is this very fact that we are to become new creations for God, that we might be pleasing gifts to Him in His kingdom. This wishing God goodness and glory is why we should strive for perfection. We want Him to possess something good when He possesses us.

They that hope in the LORD will renew their strength,
    they will soar as with eagles' wings;
They will run and not grow weary,
    walk and not grow faint. (Isaiah 40:31, *NAB*)

Charity (Love)

Many years ago I brought Communion to a man dying of cancer. He told me that he had left his wife some years before for a younger woman, with whom he had lived for several years. When he was diagnosed with cancer, the younger woman wanted no more to do with him. He asked his wife if she would take him back, and she did.

The man's wife took care of him until he died. That is a classic example of the virtue of charity.

The *Catechism* teaches, "Charity is the theological virtue by which we love God above all things for his own sake, and our neighbor as ourselves for the love of God" (CCC, #1822). This, of course, comes from the two great commandments of love that Jesus taught when asked what was necessary to attain eternal life: "You shall love the Lord your God with all your heart, and with all your soul, and with all your strength, and with all your mind; and your neighbor as yourself" (Luke 10:27). The word for *love* in the original Greek text is the verb *agapao*, which is derived from *agape*.

It seems that the meaning of this love is a giving of self for the good of the beloved without conditions. This is the way God loves us, and it is this love we must learn and make a habit in order to be ready to live in the kingdom. It is not an indiscriminate self-giving but a benevolent one. Another, simpler way of describing it is, to make other people's lives better regardless of their merits.

Jesus showed us a new kind of love when he prayed for those who crucified Him. He empowers us to love friend *and* enemy:

> You have heard that it was said, "You shall love your neighbor and
> hate your enemy." But I say to you, Love your enemies and pray for

those who persecute you, so that you may be sons of your Father who is in heaven; for he makes his sun rise on the evil and on the good, and sends rain on the just and on the unjust. For if you love those who love you, what reward have you? Do not even the tax collectors do the same? And if you salute only your brethren, what more are you doing than others? Do not even the Gentiles do the same? You, therefore, must be perfect, as your heavenly Father is perfect. (Matthew 5:43–48)

What an amazing development, this love of enemies. Jesus has taught us how to love as God loves, and loving one's enemies is, it seems, the key measure of our perfection.

What is self-love then? Not, as some have suggested, self-esteem but a concern for our own good. C.S. Lewis calls this "need love." This would include things like getting adequate sleep, nutrition, recreation as well as satisfying our spiritual needs, which are primary. Taking adequate care of ourselves (without pampering) is part of the virtue of humility. While it is true that the saints denied themselves all sorts of things to make reparation for sins, some (including Saint Bernard and Saint John Vianney) had to cut back on their penances because they exceeded prudence and made themselves sick. Prudence, as we will see in the next chapter, is not optional for the Christian.

Loving our neighbor for God's sake gives real power to our love. It means that we can love others unconditionally, since we are not dependent on a human reward. When we love others for God's sake, God assures us a reward. Thus we can persevere indefinitely in the love of a troublesome spouse or others since we are both empowered and rewarded by God.

This, no doubt, is what moved Saint Monica to love her philandering husband for so many years before her charity and kindness converted him; and it empowered Blessed Anna-Maria Taigi to love her rough, angry husband. Both chose to seek their fulfillment not from their spouses but from God. And God ended up giving them fulfillment from both sources.

Love must never be separated from the cross. Blessed Mother Teresa of Calcutta said, "Love, to be true, has to hurt."[16] Bishop Sheen would ask rhetorically if we had any scars from our loving. To love someone often means to surrender our will to their good, and that is where the cross begins.

We should never stop trying to grow in love. God revealed to Saint Catherine of Siena how He works in the soul to attain this end: "The soul is never so perfect in this life that she cannot attain to a higher perfection of love."[17]

"So faith, hope, love abide, these three; but the greatest of these is love" (1 Corinthians 13:13).

. . . . .

CHAPTER SEVENTEEN

Prudence, Justice and Fortitude

There are four cardinal, or hinge, virtues. These are the four main virtues of the moral life upon which all the other virtues depend. They include justice, fortitude and temperance, but prudence is the first.

Prudence

A couple once went to see a priest because they wanted to marry. They had known each other for just six months and were both in their late teens. The priest asked if they knew how slim their chances of success were. They admitted that they might be one in twenty. However, they assured the priest that they were the one in twenty who would succeed.

The priest asked them if perhaps all those who had failed had believed they were the one in twenty. The couple conceded that point but said they really *were* the one in twenty. The priest urged them to take some more time before taking this step, and they agreed under duress, but it was clear that they had no intention of doing so.

This is a classical example of what prudence is *not*.

Prudence, according to the Catholic *Catechism*, is "the virtue that disposes practical reason to discern our true good in every circumstance and to choose the right means of achieving it.... Prudence is 'right reason in action,' writes St. Thomas Aquinas, following Aristotle" (CCC, #1806, quoting St. Thomas Aquinas, *STh* II-II, 47, 2). It is the virtue that guides us to act reasonably.

Prudence is what inspires me to repay the hundred dollars I borrowed from Charlie last week; justice is what compels me to pay it. Prudence is what inspires me to decide it's time to get to bed; fortitude compels me to go to bed when I'd rather stay up and watch a ball game. And prudence tells me two servings of Thanksgiving turkey are enough; temperance compels me to stop eating.

Prudence requires us to think before acting. Legalism is a way people avoid thinking, by sticking to laws whether they apply or not. Situation ethics is the opposite extreme, whereby people think too much, denying moral absolutes and deciding right and wrong based on subjective opinion.

Prudence also enables us to see that we need not accept evil mixed with the good in our recreation. For example, we need not partake of entertainment that includes bad language, illicit sex or other evils. Some, especially the young, argue, "Well, there is a lot of good material in some of these movies!" In response the analogy is made of the person who made brownies with the best of ingredients but added only one tablespoon of dog excrement. "Would you eat them?" To the best of my knowledge, no one has yet volunteered to try such brownies. So, it seems we are more careful about what enters our stomach than what enters our soul.

There are many analogous recreational activities, such as watching tainted television shows; attending parties that will involve excessive drinking, drugs or other harmful things; smoking and reading books with objectionable passages. Those who are truly striving for holiness know that there are enough good forms of recreation that we need not compromise with the evil of the world. With a little creativity we can find these activities, such as sports, religious social activities and good movies and books. Not everything that is fun is sinful or fattening.

Of course, even good recreation can be overdone. If we are playing golf or tennis at every opportunity, regardless of our obligations, we are not being prudent (or temperate); we are being selfish.

Justice: Giving What Is Due

A woman I know bought something in a grocery store, and when she returned home, she discovered she had been undercharged. So the next time she went to that store, she pointed out the error to the store manager and paid him the twenty dollars she owed. He was so surprised and delighted that he invited her to take a couple pies as a gift. This woman acted in justice.

As a boy I took music lessons, and I paid for all but the last lesson. I fell into the worldly attitude, "If I can get away with it, I'll forget it." However, the teacher was my friend's father, and every time I saw him, he reminded me of the debt. I'm sure he didn't need the money, but he wanted me to learn justice. In the end I got the money and paid him. I learned more from his insistence on justice than I did from the lessons.

> Justice is the moral virtue that consists in the constant and firm will to give [our] due to God and neighbor. Justice toward God is called the 'virtue of religion.' Justice toward men disposes [us] to respect the rights of [others] and to establish in human relationships the harmony that promotes equity with regard to persons and to the common good. (CCC, #1807)

Put simply, justice involves giving what is due.

How important is justice? Very important. Sacred Scripture refers more than eight hundred times to "justice" and the "just man," the latter meaning "the good, the holy man." Cicero declared, "Good men are so called chiefly from their justice."[1]

A modern question of justice has to do with the unauthorized copying of music, movies and computer programs. Do not those who created these things have a right to some recompense? Indeed they do. It is unjust to share these things with others without permission.

This may come as a shock to some, which only shows how easily we can let justice slide. Of course, the possibilities of magnetic media are relatively new, and some have never considered them in the light of justice. But it's time we do.

There are several parts of justice. We will consider four: piety, obedience, gratitude and truthfulness.

Piety

Piety is showing the honor and veneration due to God, parents and country—in other words, to anyone who provides for our well-being and governance. The veneration due to God is called religion.

Saint Augustine taught that the word *religion* came from the Latin *religare*, meaning "to bind up." So in religion we bind ourselves to God in worship, adoration and reverence. Since God has created us and given us everything we have, we *owe* Him our prayer, our worship, our participation in the Mass and our contributions to the Church and to the poor.

Part of religious piety is to dress up for Mass. Does Sacred Scripture say anything about this? It does! "Worship the LORD in holy attire" (1 Chronicles 16:29; Psalm 29:2; 96:9). What does the Church say? "Bodily demeanor (gestures, clothing) ought to convey the respect, solemnity, and joy of this moment when Christ becomes our guest [in holy Communion]" (CCC, #1387). Devotees of John Paul II's Theology of the Body should have no problem with this, since one of his main points was that what we do with the body is important.

Genuflecting should be included under piety as well. "At the name of Jesus, every knee should bend, of those in heaven, on earth and beneath the earth" (Philippians 2:10, author's translation). Our long tradition of genuflecting before the Eucharist in the tabernacle or monstrance is based on this passage.[2] A half genuflection in public, on the other hand, seems irreverent, so those who cannot genuflect might do better to simply bow profoundly, as is custom in the Eastern rite.

Another aspect of piety is to make a sign of reverence before receiving Holy Communion. In the United States the bishops have asked that we bow our heads before stepping up to receive.

As for our contributions to the Church and to the poor, how much should we give?

As we saw earlier, the answer is broadly given in Scripture. In the Old Testament it is recommended that we give one-tenth of our income back to the Lord (see Deuteronomy 14:28–29; Numbers 18:23–24).

I visited a young couple for dinner several years ago. They told me how both of them had escaped from a sinful life to find the Lord and had given their lives over to Him entirely. They resolved when they were married that they would give 10 percent of everything to the Lord.

They debated at one point whether they should give 10 percent of their net income, after taxes, or 10 percent of their gross income. Their priest advisor answered their question with a question: "Do you want your blessings to be net or gross?" They settled on 10 percent of their gross income.

As I was having dinner with this lovely couple and their three children in a cramped apartment, it occurred to me that something was amiss. I thought, "If they have been so generous with the Lord, you would think He would provide them with better living quarters."

Then the wife told me that they had just bought a wonderful house at a great price in a very nice neighborhood, with a marvelous deal on the finances. That completed the picture, I thought, God is always far more generous with us than we are with Him. After all, He promised a hundredfold (see Matthew 19:29).

Piety toward human beings involves honoring parents and country. So patriotism is a part of the virtue of piety, a part of justice.

Obedience
Obedience is another part of justice, and it is one of the most important virtues for the spiritual life. Saint Gregory the Great said, "Obedience should be practiced, not out of servile fear, but from a sense of charity, not through fear of punishment, but through love of justice."[3] So obedience should stem from love, as should all the virtues, since love "is the *form of [all] the virtues*" (CCC, #1827)

Alas, some are quite proud of their obedience. This undermines the grace they would receive if it were practiced out of love, and they even can give obedience a bad name. It should be love, founded on humility, that moves us to obey.

When Teresa of Ávila was trying to figure out whether to found her next convent in Madrid or Seville, her spiritual director told her to ask the Lord in prayer. The Lord told her to go to Madrid. When she spoke to her director again, he ordered her to go to Seville. She obeyed her director.

The director later discovered what the Lord had said to her and asked why she had obeyed him rather than the Lord. She answered, "Faith tells me that what Your Reverence commands me is the will of God, and I have no assurance that revelations are." Sometime later the Lord appeared to her and told her she had done the right thing, so much did He value obedience to her superiors. He told her He now wanted her to go to Seville.[4]

Saint Philip Neri said, "A soul possessed of this spirit of obedience can not be lost; a soul devoid of this spirit can not be saved."[5] Jesus said to Saint Faustina, "You give Me greater glory by a single act of obedience than by long prayers and mortification."[6]

We should note that obedience, even for a religious who has vowed obedience, does not apply to an immoral command. Our first obedience must be to God and His law.

For the laity obedience to the moral teachings of the Church, liturgical norms, such as those governing the proper reception of Communion, and obedience to traffic laws[7] are examples of exercising this grace-giving virtue. We must also be obedient to our duties in life: for example, schoolwork for a student, care of children for a parent, doing one's work for an employee. The virtue of obedience prompts us to do the things we are obliged to do before doing the things we'd like to do.

Gratitude and Truthfulness

In our affluent Western world, we certainly have a lot to be grateful for. Yet we often forget to give thanks. For example, we may say grace before meals, but do we say grace after meals? ("We give You thanks for all Your benefits, Almighty God, who lives and reigns forever and ever. And may the souls of the faithful departed through the mercy of God rest in peace. Amen.")

There are those who are constantly grateful for every little thing in their life, and then there are those who are constantly complaining. Which do you think are happier?

Justice also obliges us to speak the truth. Does that mean we are always to tell all the truth we know? Not at all. We may withhold information if the person to whom we are speaking has no right to it. We may either refuse to answer or evade a question or say something that is true in one sense but not in another. Thomas Aquinas wrote, "It is not lawful to tell a lie in order to deliver another from any danger whatever. Nevertheless it is lawful to hide the truth prudently, by keeping it back, as Augustine says."[8]

For example, if a woman walks into her workplace wearing a very ugly hat and asks her employee how he likes it, he might reply, "It's out of this world."

Of course, if a parent asks a child about his homework or how he did on an exam, the child must answer truthfully. A parent has a right to that information.

Fortitude: Difficult Yeses

When Thomas More refused to sign documents declaring King Henry VIII head of the Catholic Church in England and his children by Anne Boleyn legitimate, he was found guilty of treason. After suffering for fifteen months as a prisoner in the Tower of London, Thomas More was beheaded on July 6, 1535. He was beatified in 1886 and canonized in 1935. His willingness to die for his faith and the truth is considered a classic example of fortitude.

What is the virtue of fortitude? It is the virtue that empowers a person to overcome great difficulties to do what is good. Josef

Pieper said: "Fortitude presupposes vulnerability; without vulnerability there is no possibility of fortitude. An angel cannot be brave, because he is not vulnerable. To be brave actually means to be able to suffer injury. Because man is by nature vulnerable, he can be brave."[9]

So in order to practice the virtue of fortitude, we must be able to be injured, and the worst bodily injury is death. According to Saint Thomas Aquinas, fortitude is ultimately concerned with the danger of death in a battle to do good.[10] Fortitude is the virtue that enables the Christian to bear martyrdom.

Saint Felicity gave birth to a baby while she was in prison awaiting execution for being a Christian. She cried out in great pain while she was in labor, and the other prisoners asked how she would endure her cruel martyrdom if she struggled so much in childbirth. Her reply was, "Today it is I who suffer in giving birth, but then it will be Another who will suffer in me, because I shall suffer for him."[11]

We need the virtue of fortitude to function in our everyday lives, sometimes just to get out of bed in the morning. One critical area where fortitude is needed is that of communication, especially about displeasure over another's behavior. We risk an angry response or even losing a friendship when we express it. However, if we do not communicate our displeasure, our relationship with the other person may gradually disintegrate.

Fortitude is extremely important for the spiritual life, for two reasons. First, purgation from our sins and vices is a painful process that we must undergo to get close to God. And second, we must endure the dryness of finding no consolation in prayer, when God withdraws and invites us to let go of all His gifts and cling to Him alone.

Fortitude can be called the virtue of difficult yeses. Our next chapter is on the virtue of difficult noes, temperance. Both these cardinal virtues help us make decisions that go against the grain of our culture for the sake of our faith.

. . . . .

CHAPTER EIGHTEEN

Temperance

What do workaholics, computerholics, sex addicts, alcoholics, TV addicts, overeaters, addictive gamblers and love addicts have in common? They are all missing the virtue of temperance.

Temperance is the habit of moderating the attracting appetites in accord with reason. Now, the attracting appetites are many, but those involving food, drink and sex are generally considered the most powerful. It is no accident that these strong appetites are most closely associated with human flourishing. Eating and drinking ensure individual survival; sex ensures survival of the entire human race.

When our appetites are not ordered properly—that is, when they are not governed by right reason—they become like spoiled little brats. They want their own way; they do not know when to stop; and the more they get, the more they want. And like children, disordered appetites can only be corrected by being restrained.

But restraining children is not enough, and neither is it enough to simply restrain the appetites. If you restrain children without ever training them, they will merely wait for a time when you are not there and then explode in a binge of self-gratification. In other words, children must be taught to see the good reasons for their restraints, so they can make those restraints their own.

So it is with our appetites. A young man might curb his sexual appetite by simply saying, "No, no, no," over and over again, thereby repressing it. But after doing well for six weeks or so, all of a sudden he might go wild. That's called "white-knuckle chastity."

The appetites, say Aristotle and Saint Thomas, must be treated politically. That is, they must be persuaded. Pope John Paul II said that the will must be "confronted by a value which fully explains the necessity for containing impulses aroused by carnal desire and sensuality. Only as this value gradually takes possession of the mind and the will does the will become calm and free itself from a characteristic sense of loss."[1]

That is, the appetites, whether sexual or other, must be convinced by reason. In this way they become trained to act in accord with right reason habitually. Only then can a person claim to have the virtue of temperance.

In the case of the young man, he should say, "No, and here's why." Thomas Aquinas taught that the appetites listen not only to reason but to imagination and the senses as well. Eventually, through perseverance, the inordinate appetites just give up and admit, "OK, OK, you're right. I give in. That won't make me happy."

Success at saying no to the appetites when appropriate is continence, or self-control, whereas training the appetites not to get stirred up at all when inappropriate is temperance. Self-control, then, involves a struggle, whereas temperance forgoes an attractive but immoral object with serenity.

As an example of how to "convert" the appetites, a young man some years ago began at my request to read the following list of reasons why he should be chaste:

1. Sex is holy, not a plaything. It should never be trivialized.
2. Created in the image of God, I can live by reason, not just by urges (as the animals do).

3. Persons are to be loved, not used as objects of enjoyment.
4. I must not treat persons as objects, even in the mind, lest I become a user of persons in practice.
5. Unchaste activity destroys my most precious friendship, that with God, the source of all happiness.
6. Unchaste activity brings pleasure but not happiness.

After reading these several times a day for a year, the young man found peace. He had no more struggles to be chaste. Another young man was able to just about eliminate his pornography habit after reading these statements for a couple years.

This method of giving yourself the reasons to avoid harmful things can be applied to any of the appetites—for food, drink, a dysfunctional love, gambling and so on. Ultimately we are more attracted to the truth than to pleasure.

Temperance in Action
Now, there are several parts of temperance: abstinence, sobriety, chastity and purity. We already considered the way to achieve chastity, but I'd like to say a little more.

The *Catechism* tells us, "Sexual pleasure is morally disordered when sought for itself, isolated from its procreative and unitive purposes" (CCC, #2351). This statement defines the norm for chastity: Sexual pleasure that *respects* its procreative and unitive purposes. The unitive purpose implies the celebration of the existing marital love covenant of the couple: Sexual pleasure may be sought only in marriage. And the procreative purpose means that the sexual act is open to children, regardless of the intention of the (married) couple. In other words, it must be a complete, uncontracepted marital act.

Abstinence is the virtue of consuming food and drink in accord with right reason. So the diabetic who avoids sweets consistently has the virtue of abstinence. So does the person who stays away from milk products because of an allergy. So does the person who never overindulges in food or alcohol. We cannot be holy if we overindulge in anything. (It seems abstinence is not a terribly popular virtue in our Western world.)

With the virtue of abstinence comes fasting. Fasting, according to Saint Thomas Aquinas, has three purposes. The first is to control the disordered desires of the flesh—not just the desire for food and drink but all the desires of the flesh, including sexual desires. Saint Jerome explained that "Venus is cold when Ceres and Bacchus are not there."[2] In other words, lust is diminished when a person fasts from food and drink.

The second reason for fasting is to free us to reflect on our eternal goal. If we are thinking about food all the time, it is hard to keep our attention on the spiritual life.

The third reason for fasting is to make reparation for sin, one's own or the sins of the world. Saint Augustine summed up the value of fasting: it "cleanses the soul, raises the mind, subjects one's flesh to the spirit, renders the heart contrite and humble, scatters the clouds of concupiscence, quenches the fire of lust, kindles the true light of chastity."[3]

Fasting is not optional for the Christian. Jesus told the Pharisees, "The days will come, when the bridegroom is taken away from them, and then they will fast in that day" (Mark 2:20). Saint Thomas Aquinas wrote, "Fasting is useful as atoning for and preventing sin, and as raising the mind to spiritual things. And everyone is bound by the natural dictate of reason to practice fasting as far as it is necessary for these purposes."[4]

And according to Canon Law, all Christians are obliged to fast. "The divine law binds all the Christian faithful to do penance each in his or her own way."[5]

Fasting applies not only to food but to other enjoyable things, such as listening to music and watching television. Fasting, or doing penance, is primarily about denying the will, not just the body. The Lord said to Saint Catherine of Siena, "[The person] who desires for My sake to mortify his body with many penances, and not his own will, did not give Me much pleasure."[6]

And of course, fasting must always be done with prudence. Fasting to the point of ruining your health is not pleasing to God, as Saint Bernard learned the hard way.

Detachment

Detachment is an extremely important element of holiness, and it is part of temperance. To be detached in a spiritual context is to enjoy things without being dependent on them.

An attachment is something or someone we feel we *must* have in order to be happy, whether it be a computer game, a car, certain foods, a boyfriend or girlfriend. What the Christian needs to be happy is God and whatever He gives us for the moment. Every attachment is in competition with God. Everything in second place is a threat to what is first.

One of the demonic ploys is to get us to attach ourselves to the pleasures of this world, so we will forget about the next. To be worldly means to be so concerned about this world that we have little time for God, for loving Him and our neighbor. Even success can be a dangerous thing if it distracts us from God or becomes our primary goal. Our citizenship is in heaven (Philippians 3:20) not here, where we are just travelers.

Moderation in the use of television is of great importance in this age, especially for the young. One young mother got rid of the family television as an experiment. Within two weeks she saw a great improvement in the behavior of her children. The TV never returned.

Television seems to have an addictive power over many. Unfortunately, it often has little to offer. When I was ordained I resolved to never watch television except on Sundays and feast days. What a blessing that has been! Because of television's addictive power, I do recommend designating most days as TV-free days if you want to become holy.

Using computers, especially the Internet, is another good that should be moderated by temperance. I use alarm software to regulate my use of the computer, with alarms going off at prayer times, dinnertimes, bedtime and so on.

The use of cellular phones needs to be tempered as well, especially among teenagers. One young woman overran her minutes one month by $2,000. Her parents made her pay every penny, and she learned some temperance the hard way.

The trouble with these seemingly harmless addictions to TV, computers and phones is that they develop a mind-set, especially among the young, of seeking pleasure without reference to reason. Those who run free with the use of TV or computers when they are young are good candidates for addiction to alcohol, drugs and sex when they are older.

Workaholism is another area of addiction that needs to be moderated by temperance. Some feel so fulfilled by their work that they neglect family, health and even a normal social life. Again, reason must govern for the Christian.

Detachment gives us a beautiful way to live. We possess our

things; they don't possess us. We are not always worried about losing what we have but are happy to have them for now. If we lose possessions we try to forget about them and stay focused on the Lord. Our attitude should be that of Job: "Naked I came from my mother's womb, and naked shall I return; the LORD gave, and the LORD has taken away; blessed be the name of the LORD" (Job 1:21).

Being detached from a friend, a girlfriend or even a spouse sounds cold. But to be detached spiritually means to love others primarily for their sake and especially for God's sake, not for our own sake. It means we love people not for the pleasure they give us but for their good and to please God. Granted, we get pleasure from loving people, and we should enjoy that pleasure, but we should never cling to it, making it a priority. To make pleasure the most important thing in any endeavor is to be a hedonist.

Alas, many of us have been hedonists from time to time, but hedonism is not a part of holiness. We should constantly remind ourselves that happiness comes from love, not pleasure.

Continence, Humility and Modesty

Now, there are several virtues that are associated with temperance or are means of attaining it. We will consider three: continence—that is, self-control—humility and modesty.

Continence, as we mentioned earlier, is that self-control one needs to keep from falling for an unreasonable desire while developing the virtue of temperance. One exercises continence by looking at the pecan pie covered with ice cream and thinking, "Oh, I would love to eat that, but I really shouldn't. The doctor told me to lose twenty pounds, but it looks *so* good. No, no, no! I *am* going to lose weight; and I'm going to start right now." That's continence.

With temperance you look at that same piece of pie and think, "Nice, but not for me. I've said no the last fifty times, and I'll say no this time too. My diet is working, and I feel good about it. No problem!"

Humility is part of temperance too, since it involves moderating the appetite for praise. We need the affirmation of praise from time to time, but we need food, too. We should be detached from both.

So humility helps us be *detached* from praise, not depending on it for our happiness. If we love we will get praise, and that's fine, but if we don't get praise, we still love because it's loving that makes us happy. When the humble person is praised, he need not deny he has done something good, but he will give most of the credit to God.

Humility, of course, is an elusive virtue. You struggle to attain it, and once you say to yourself, "Ah, at last I am humble," you've lost it! The person who is truly humble is deeply aware of his tendency to be proud. This is the paradox of humility.

A young woman confessed to Bishop Sheen that she was "the worst girl in the city of New York." Sheen replied, "You are not…; the worst girl in the city of New York says that she is the best girl in the city of New York."[7]

Modesty is like humility but pertains to less attractive goods. The desire we most often associate with immodesty is that of being noticed or highly regarded. One who is modest does not parade his assets or accomplishments; rather he realizes that any good that he has or has done is in large part a grace from God. Yes, he acknowledges what he has done well, but he doesn't seek notice or praise. His attitude is, "This is good, but will it help me get to the kingdom? If so, thanks be to God!"

Modesty of dress serves chastity, and it is especially important for women. When a woman dresses modestly and with class, she is far more likely to be treated as a person, as someone with dignity. Girls should be alerted to this from a young age. Alas, there are many good women who have barely a clue as to how men are interiorly responding to the way they dress.[8]

So temperance is an important virtue involving difficult noes to pleasant things. But a no to pleasure can be a yes to reason, and the dignity of a human person includes the ability to live by reason, in the image of God. If we hope to live with Him, we need to have this virtue and all the others as well.

Living Simply

Every Christian is called to live simply, which is another part of temperance. Father Thomas Dubay wrote in *Happy Are You Poor*, "Scripture scholars seem to be of one mind...that most New Testament texts that deal with poverty as an ideal are meant to be applied to all who follow Christ."[9]

The most important example of simplicity is that of the Holy Family. Jesus was born in a stable. A stable! The Son of God! Was that a fluke, or was there a message there—namely, as Saint Francis understood, that *we* should live humbly, simply? Jesus encouraged that: "Blessed are you poor, for yours is the kingdom of God" (Luke 6:20).

If we read about the saints, we see that much of their credibility came from the fact that they lived in poverty. In their very lives they taught detachment from material goods and the importance of living for the kingdom. This gives the gospel a richness that the world can admire. Even the media—yes, the media!—could hardly resist little Mother Teresa of Calcutta, a poor sister who cared for the poor.

Jesus warned of the dangers of riches: "[W]oe to you that are rich, for you have received your consolation" (Luke 6:24); "[I]t will be hard for a rich man to enter the kingdom of heaven" (Matthew 19:23).

Why is the Lord so hard on the rich? Saint Ignatius of Loyola wrote in the *Spiritual Exercises*: "[The devil] bids [his demons] first to tempt men with the lust of riches, ... that they may thereby more easily gain the empty honor of the world, and then come to unbounded pride. The first step in his snare is that of riches, the second honor, and the third pride."[10] Pride is the root of every vice.

Paul tells us there is great danger in riches:

There is great gain in godliness with contentment; for we brought nothing into the world, and we cannot take anything out.... [I]f we have food and clothing, with these we shall be content. But those who desire to be rich fall into temptation, into a snare, into many senseless and hurtful desires that plunge men into ruin and destruction. For the love of money is the root of all evils; it is through this craving that some have wandered away from the faith. (1 Timothy 6:6–10)

James has strong words for the rich as well: "For the sun rises with its scorching heat and withers the grass; its flower falls, and its beauty perishes. So will the rich man fade away in the midst of his pursuits" (James 1:11).

There is another reason not to be rich: We are responsible for the poor. We cannot live in relative luxury while the poor do not have enough to eat. "[I]f anyone has the world's goods and sees his brother in need, yet closes his heart against him, how does God's love abide in him? Little children, let us not love in word or speech but in deed and in truth" (1 John 3:17).

Saint Ambrose said, "You are not making a gift of your possessions to the poor person. You are handing over to him what is his. For what has been given in common for the use of all, you have [claimed for] yourself. The world is given to all, and not only to the rich."[11] And Jesus said, "[A]s you did it to one of the least of these my brethren, you did it to me" (Matthew 25:40).

Well, "I'm not really rich," some will say. "I live comfortably, but I'm not rich." But those of us in the Western world are some of the richest people who have ever lived. And we have a tremendous opportunity to give to those who are less fortunate.

Pope John Paul II pointed out, "Children must grow up with a correct attitude of freedom with regard to material goods, by adopting a simple and austere lifestyle and being fully convinced that 'man is more precious for what he is than for what he has.'"[12] Parents need to exercise caution in how much they buy their children but also show them the joys of "a simple and austere lifestyle."

Your goal as a Christian is to adopt a standard of living that is based on your faith commitment rather than your income. To this end you must live well within your means (meaning buying a house and car you can *easily* afford), avoid pouring money down the drain through credit card debt, keep your house and car in good repair and shrink your appetite for buying. Not only will you be living simply, but you'll always feel rich!

. . . . .

CHAPTER NINETEEN

The Fruits of the Holy Spirit

Many years ago a young man came to see me, having returned to the Church about six months prior. He told me he had some Catholic friends who seemed to have a very strong faith and to be consistently loving. "How can I get that kind of faith and love?"

I told him that faith, firm faith, as Saint Thomas Aquinas calls it, is a fruit of the Holy Spirit, as is love (charity). I explained, "The fruits are the last things to appear on a tree, so it will take you time to develop these as you grow in the spiritual life. It may take years, but it's worth it."

The fruits of the Holy Spirit are a kind of barometer to indicate how we are doing in our spiritual journey. For example, if we are able to wait patiently for things to happen, this is a sign of spiritual advancement. Perhaps the acid test of patience is when we are behind the wheel of a car, and the person ahead is inexplicably crawling along.

Kindness

A well-known moral theologian told of the advice he received from his father on his wedding day. His father called him aside and told him to remember one word in his marriage: kindness. He thought little of it at the time, but as his marriage progressed he saw more and more that it was great advice. How many marriages could be saved if both parties were consistently kind?

How pleasant it is when a person greets strangers with a kind smile. There are many people walking around in our world who are hurting a great deal inside for various reasons. What a boost it can be for one of them to receive a warm greeting from a stranger. Christians should be in the habit of giving such a greeting.

Perhaps the greatest challenge is showing kindness to our enemies or to those who have hurt us. Saint Thérèse of Lisieux lived with a nun who always rubbed her the wrong way. Whenever she saw her she would smile, pray for her and offer God all her virtues and merits. She showed her every kindness whenever she could.

One day the sister asked, "Sister Thérèse, will you please tell me what attracts you so much to me? You give me such a charming smile whenever we meet."

Thérèse answered that it was because she was "happy to see her." She was indeed happy: happy to love someone she didn't like.[1]

One person went to visit a relative who could be quite difficult at times. When things started out badly, she prayed to Saint Thérèse to help her be kind to the relative. The next morning the relative became quite pleasant!

It is most important for parents to be kind to their children. They should discipline them fairly, but even in punishment they should try to be kind. Teenagers often can deal with the punishment they receive from their parents but not the silent treatment they may endure for a week or two afterward.

One mother complained that her son's grandmother would go to her son's room and console him when he was sent there for punishment. When she asked her priest what she should do about it, he replied, "Wait till she is finished, and then go up and console him yourself."

Kindness, as a virtue, need not require thought in every situation. Once you make it a habit—with the help of the Holy Spirit—it comes naturally.

Sarcasm is a vice opposed to kindness, since it is caustic witticism. There is always a bite to sarcasm. To live out the virtue of kindness, we should eliminate all sarcasm. Facetiousness, on the other hand, is a harmless witticism, a humorous quip about the ironies of life.

Another destroyer of kindness is moods. When we give in to a foul mood, we are saying to everyone in our presence, in effect, "How I feel is more important than you or your comfort." The people who are cheerful almost all the time are not ordinarily mood-free; they just refuse to give in to their moods. Everyone has moods, and as something not willed, there is nothing wrong with them. But it is what we do with them that determines our virtue, our living in the Spirit.

Many presume that there are just some people who are cheerful all the time and some who are not, and that's the way it will continue to be. Not so. A number of people have exercised their will to change and become cheerful. This was the case with Saint Thérèse of Lisieux, who was melancholy as a child but through great effort (and grace) became a bubbling sanguine personality.

One of the ways I have seen people overcome their melancholy and negative personality is to begin to praise God for everything that happens in their life, good or bad. This is based in part on Romans 8:28: "We know that all things work out unto good for those who love God" (author's translation). Those who love God and believe that verse wholeheartedly can trust that, no matter what happens, good will come.

Praising God for all things is also based on the fact that by embracing crosses, we can save souls (more on this in the next chapter). I have observed many people change from being rather negative to becoming quite positive simply by making a habit of praising God in every situation.

Some claim shyness as their reason to not present a warm facade in public. It seems, however, that many people are shy until they work at overcoming it. And even shy people should be able to offer a warm smile to those they meet. Those who make a habit of that are living out the virtue of kindness and practicing Christian love.

Courtesy and Gentleness

Courtesy is another part of kindness. We read in Sacred Scripture, "Remind [the people] to be submissive to rulers and authorities, to be obedient, to be ready for any honest work, to speak evil of no one, to avoid quarreling, to be gentle, and to show perfect courtesy toward all men" (Titus 3:1–2). Saint Francis of Assisi said, "[C]ourtesy is one of the properties of God, who of His courtesy, gives His sun and rain to the just and the unjust: and courtesy is the sister of charity by which hatred is extinguished and love is cherished."[2]

There are many books written on courtesy. One I would recommend is *A Book of Courtesy* by a teaching sister, some key points of which follow:

- Be on time (habitual lateness is often a sign of pride).
- Make a habit of saying please and thank you to *everyone*, regardless of age or social status.
- Don't interrupt, and don't contradict.
- Return calls and E-mails within a day; answer invitations within a week if possible.

- If you are going to be late, call and let the host know.
- If you miss an appointment, call and apologize strongly and humbly.
- Turn cell phones off when meeting with others and in church. If you must take a call, go somewhere private. Avoid being glued to a cell phone when you are with others.[3]

We all could probably find something on this list we need to work at. It is said that good manners are a series of inconveniences to make others feel comfortable.

Gentleness is opposed to anger, which poisons many relationships. Granted, there is such a thing as just anger. Saint Thomas Aquinas wrote, "[I]f one is angry in accordance with right reason, one's anger is deserving of praise."[4] However, anger is numbered among the seven cardinal sins. Thus it is ordinarily one of the "hinge" or root sins.

In James we read:

Let every man be quick to hear, slow to speak, slow to anger, for the anger of man does not work the righteousness of God. Therefore put away all filthiness and rank growth of wickedness and receive with meekness the implanted word, which is able to save your souls....

If any one thinks he is religious, and does not bridle his tongue but deceives his heart, this man's religion is vain. (James 1:19–21, 26)

The feeling of anger is not, of course, a sin, since feelings may come over us without our willing them. But the one who cultivates the feeling of anger or acts on such a feeling in an unreasonable way is guilty of sin. Anger often stems from pride. Thus to overcome anger we should pray for the virtue of humility.

Gentleness and kindness would, it seems, preclude foul language or cursing. The mouth that receives the Lord in Holy Communion should not utter obscenities. The measure of morality, as Pope John Paul II said in *Veritatis Splendor*, is Jesus Himself. I doubt He ever said a foul word.

More Fruits

Faithfulness (*pistis* in Greek) is more than faith. It is a firm belief in Christ that is lived out, especially by acts of love. We might apply here Saint Paul's expression "faith working through love" (Galatians 5:6). It involves a commitment to Christ and implies trust and obedience, based on years of prayer and practicing the faith. In fact, prayer, the sacraments and reading the saints seem to be the best ways to deepen our faithfulness.

Charity, as a fruit of the Spirit, is a supernatural active concern for the good of all, including our enemies, and for serving God in all things. Like faithfulness, it is firm and quick in its exercise.

Goodness refers to doing what is right—that is, being a moral person. On earth there is no necessary connection between goodness and beauty. There are many outwardly beautiful people who are not good, and there are many good people who do not have beauty. But in the life to come they are one. The ugliness of those who lived evil lives on earth will be clearly seen by all, as will shine the inner beauty of those who were good. The deeper our goodness and holiness in this life, the more beautiful we will be in the next.

The fruit of joy comes from a strong relationship with God. Saint Bonaventure said, "A spiritual joy is the greatest sign of divine grace dwelling in a soul."[5] And Saint Francis of Assisi said, "[S]piritual joy is as necessary to the soul as blood is to the body."[6]

Jesus told the disciples: "As the Father has loved me, so have I loved you; abide in my love. If you keep my commandments, you will abide in my love, just as I have kept my Father's commandments and abide in his love. These things I have spoken to you, that my joy may be in you, and that your joy may be full" (John 15:9–11).

Can we find joy only in God? Spiritual joy, yes. There are other kinds of joy that stem from our interaction with the world, and these can be good—the joy of parenting, for example, or of a job well done. However, as Cardinal Newman wrote, "The true Christian rejoices in those earthly things which give joy, but in such a way as not to care for them when they go."[7]

And we Christians are to find joy in all things, including suffering. Saint Clare said, "Melancholy is the poison of devotion. When one is in tribulation, it is necessary to be more happy and more joyful because one is nearer to God."[8]

The Christian does not wait for a good feeling in order to be spiritually joyful. Saint John Vianney said, "It is always springtime in the heart that loves God."[9] Merlin Carothers, one of the foremost proponents of praising and thanking God in all things, wrote, "Accepting every little thing that happens with joy and thanksgiving will release the power of God in and through us, and we will soon experience a *feeling* of joy as well. But don't look for the feeling as a sign. Our praise and thanksgiving must be based on faith in God's Word, not on our feelings."[10]

If we are to have the fruits of the Spirit, we must live by the Spirit and not by feelings. According to Cardinal Newman, "We must live in sunshine, even when we sorrow."[11]

How important it is to cultivate joy! Saint Thomas Aquinas wrote, "No one can live without delight and that is why [one] deprived of spiritual joy goes over to carnal pleasures."[12] So "Rejoice in the Lord always; again I will say, Rejoice!" (Philippians 4:4).

The Peace of Christ

When Jesus rose from the dead, He appeared to his disciples and greeted them: "Peace be with you" (John 20:19). He repeated this on that visit, and then again when He came a week later. He told them to wish peace on the house of those with whom they stayed, and "if the house is worthy, let your peace come upon it; but if it is not worthy, let your peace return to you" (Matthew 10:13). And He told His disciples He was giving them a new kind of peace: "[M]y peace I give to you; not as the world gives do I give to you" (John 14:27).

The supernatural peace that Christ gives is the result of trust. And trust, in turn, is the result of drawing close to God through spiritual activities. We will consider trust more in the next chapter.

One thing that kills peace is resentment. How many people hang on to resentment about what someone did—their husband or wife, their sister or their boss. But if we bear injustices patiently and forgive all injuries (two of the spiritual works of mercy), resentment flies away, and our peace returns. If we feel resentful, we should either try to resolve it by gently asking for better behavior or embrace the injustice as a penance.

It seems that many people are constantly in turmoil. They cannot find peace because they are concerned about all sorts of things, rather than choosing "the better part," focusing on Christ (see Luke 10:42). So often we forget to live out the serenity prayer:

> God, give us grace to accept with serenity the things that cannot be changed,

courage to change the things which should be changed,
and the wisdom to distinguish the one from the other.

There is more to this prayer by Reinhold Niebuhr:

Living one day at a time,
Enjoying one moment at a time,
Accepting hardship as a pathway to peace,
Taking, as Jesus did,
This sinful world as it is,
Not as I would have it,
Trusting that You will make all things right,
If I surrender to Your will,
So that I may be reasonably happy in this life,
And supremely happy with You forever in the next.[13]

True, lasting, supernatural peace comes from God alone. Right after Saint Paul urges the Philippians to rejoice always, show others their kindness, get rid of anxiety and pray to God while thanking Him, he tells them, "And the peace of God, which passes all understanding, will keep your hearts and your minds in Christ Jesus" (Philippians 4:7). Saint Augustine believed that the very essence of heaven would be peace, and he urged us to seek that peace here as well: "[Y]ou have made us for yourself, and our heart is restless until it rests in you."[14]

. . . . .

CHAPTER TWENTY

The Shortest Way to the Kingdom

In actuality there are no shortcuts to the kingdom. The basics—prayer, the sacraments and virtue—are essential. But there are certain elements of the spiritual life that make the journey more efficient. The saints found them and have encouraged us to make use of them. Some of these we have already talked about, but their importance begs reiteration here.

There is nothing that brings us more grace than the Mass, and goodness knows we need all the grace we can get to enter the kingdom. Perhaps this is why Saint Joseph Cottelengo recommended daily Mass for everyone and said that those who do not go to daily Mass practice bad time management. Pray, pray that God will give you the grace to go to Mass every day. God will answer that prayer.

As we saw in the chapter on the spiritual works of mercy, we may help the dead a great deal by offering indulgences for them. But we may also offer indulgences for ourselves. Either aids us on the path to holiness.

We can receive a partial indulgence for listening attentively to the homily at Mass and each time we make the Sign of the Cross. We can receive a partial indulgence for humbly making a pious invocation (a prayer) while carrying out our life's duties; by helping those in need; by abstaining from something good in a spirit of penance or by giving witness to the faith to others.[1] And there are any number of prayers that gain a partial indulgence.[2]

Devotion to Mary

Apparently the Lord loves it when we pay attention to his mother and come to Him through her. Pope Pius XII once called devotion to Mary "a sign of 'predestination' according to the opinion of holy men."[3] In other words, this devotion is an indication that a person is on the way to the kingdom.

Saint John Vianney seemed to know the whereabouts of souls who had died. The saint once told a widow whom he had never met and who had lost her husband to suicide, "He is saved! ... He is in Purgatory.... Between the parapet of the bridge and the water he had time to make an act of contrition. Our Blessed Lady obtained that grace for him.... Though your husband professed to have no religion, he sometimes joined you in [the Marian] prayers; this merited for him the grace of repentance...."[4]

Mary is the kind of friend we want to have!

Saint Louis de Montfort suggested a long list of ways to live out our devotion to Mary. Here are a few:

- Offer her works of praise, love and gratitude.
- Call on her with a joyful heart.
- Do things to please her.
- Honor her above all the other saints.
- Meditate on her virtues, privileges and actions.
- Pray the rosary.
- Wear the scapular.
- Sing hymns to her.
- Decorate her altars.[5]

And another, from Maximilian Kolbe and others: Give away miraculous medals.

There should be no question, based on the example of the saints, that devotion to Mary is the most efficient way to draw close to her Son. She brought Him forth to us. She is eager to bring us forth to Him.

The Rosary

Of particular note is the rosary. We already talked about this prayer in chapter six, but I'd like to emphasize here its benefits.

Bishop Fulton Sheen wrote:

> The Rosary is the meeting ground of the uneducated and the learned; the place where the simple love grows in knowledge and where the knowing mind grows in love....
>
> The Rosary is the book of the blind, where souls see and there enact the greatest drama of love the world has ever known; it is the book of the simple, which initiates them into mysteries and knowledge more satisfying than the education of other men; it is the book of the aged, whose eyes close upon the shadow of this world, and open on the substance of the next. The power of the Rosary is beyond description.[6]

There are fifteen promises that Mary is said to have made to Blessed Alan de la Roche regarding those who pray the rosary. They include:

- I will deliver from purgatory souls devoted to my Rosary.
- True children of my Rosary will enjoy great glory in heaven.
- To those who propagate my Rosary I promise aid in all their necessities.
- Devotion to my Rosary is a special sign of predestination.[7]

The rosary is so effective because it brings us through Mary to the heart of Jesus. And that's where we want to be.

Humility

According to Saint Augustine, "If you ask me what is the most essential element in the teaching and morality of Jesus Christ, I would answer you: the first is humility, the second is humility, and the third is humility."[8]

Shortly before Saint Francis de Sales died, he was leaving the Visitation Sisters, and the mother superior asked him for one last piece of wisdom. He wrote three times on a piece of paper, "Humility."[9]

Humility is consistently praised in Sacred Scripture, and pride disdained: "He who is greatest among you shall be your servant; whoever exalts himself will be humbled, and whoever humbles himself will be exalted" (Matthew 23:11–12). "[H]e has scattered the proud in the imagination of their hearts, / he has put down the mighty from their thrones, / and exalted those of low degree" (Luke 1:51–52).

Humility is praised about 25 times in Scripture; the humble are praised about 48 times. Pride is held in contempt 103 times; the proud are disdained about 68 times. If there was ever a foundational virtue to strive for, it is humility.

Cardinal Merry del Val wrote a litany of humility. What follows is an abbreviated and slightly altered version of that prayer.

O Jesus! meek and humble of heart,
make my heart like unto thine.
From the desire to be esteemed, deliver me.
From the desire to be honored, deliver me.
From the desire to be praised, deliver me.
Teach me to accept humiliation,
contempt, rebukes,
being slandered, being ignored,
being insulted, being wronged
and being belittled.

Jesus, grant me the grace
that others be admired more than I;

that others be praised and I unnoticed;

that others be preferred to me in everything;

that others be holier than I, provided I become as holy as I
should;

that I might imitate the patience and obedience of Your mother,
Mary. Amen.[10]

Humility: don't leave home without it.

Obedience

We read in 1 Samuel: "Behold, to obey is better than sacrifice,
/ and to listen than the fat of rams" (1 Samuel 15:22). And in
Psalm 40, "I delight to do your will, O my God; / your law is
within my heart" (Psalm 40:8).

Saint Alphonsus Rodriguez wrote, "To pick up a [piece of]
straw from the ground through obedience is more meritorious
than to preach, to fast, to use the discipline to blood, and to make
long prayers, of one's own will."[11] And Teresa of Avila, when
tempted to disobey her spiritual director and perform heroic acts
of penance in imitation of a recently deceased holy woman of the
town, was told by our Lord, "You know all the penances she prac-
tised? I appreciate your obedience much more."[12]

The Lord appeared to Saint Margaret Mary Alacoque once
and said: "I am the absolute Master of My gifts as also of My
creatures, and nothing will be able to prevent Me from carrying
out My designs. Therefore, not only do I desire that [you
should] do what [your] Superiors command, but also that [you
should] do nothing of all that I order [you] without their con-
sent. I love obedience, and without it no one can please Me."[13]

Saint Thérèse of Lisieux performed few great penances, but
she obeyed just about everyone, including those who had no
authority over her. Saint Francis of Assisi strove for a similar
obedience.

The story is told of a monk in one of the early centuries who was writing something when the bell rang for prayer. It was discovered later that he stopped writing not in the middle of a sentence but in the middle of a word!

How does a layperson obey? Keep the traffic laws, the Church's liturgical laws and the moral laws, and fulfill the duties of your state in life.

Mercy and Trust

Our blessed Lord appeared to Saint Faustina, an obscure nun in Poland, from 1931 to 1938, to announce that mercy was God's greatest attribute and to have her spread a new devotion to His mercy. He showed her an image of Himself that He wanted painted and promised that whoever venerated this image would not perish. The image was of Jesus with two rays coming out of His heart, a red one representing the blood and a white one the water that poured out when His heart was pierced on Calvary. It is said that these rays symbolize the Eucharist and baptism.

Jesus told Saint Faustina, "I desire that priests proclaim this great mercy of Mine towards souls of sinners.... I want to pour [the flames of mercy] out upon these souls."[14] He further told her that we would not know peace until we place trust in His mercy.

On September 13, 1935, Jesus gave Sister Faustina a new chaplet of prayers to pacify His anger, the Divine Mercy Chaplet. It begins with an Our Father, Hail Mary and Apostles' Creed. Then, using the rosary, on the Our Father beads we recite the prayer,

> Eternal Father,
> I offer You the Body and Blood,
> Soul and Divinity
> of Your dearly beloved Son,
> Our Lord Jesus Christ,

in atonement for our sins
and those of the whole world.

On the Hail Mary beads we pray:

For the sake of His sorrowful Passion,
have mercy on us and on the whole world.

And at the end of the five decades we pray three times:

Holy God,
Holy Mighty One,
Holy Immortal One,
have mercy on us and on the whole world.[15]

In November 1936 Jesus told Sister Faustina that whoever said the chaplet would be received into His mercy, especially just before death. At that time He would defend them "as My own glory."[16] He called for a Feast of Divine Mercy, which Pope John Paul II designated as the Sunday after Easter in 2000. Jesus promised that anyone who would confess and go to Communion on that day would receive a full remission of all punishment for sins.[17] It is said that confession during Lent, in preparation for Easter, fulfills the confession condition.[18]

At another point Jesus insisted that those who seek mercy should show it to others. This would include works of mercy and forgiveness, which Jesus said are essential if we wish to receive forgiveness (see Matthew 6:14–15). [19]

When our Lord gave the image of Divine Mercy to Sister Faustina, he indicated he wanted the caption at the bottom to read, "Jesus, I trust in You." He told her at one point, "Encourage souls to place great trust in My fathomless mercy. Let the weak, sinful soul have no fear to approach Me, for even if it had more sins than there are grains of sand in the world, all will be drowned in the unmeasurable depths of My mercy."[20]

Later He told her, "The graces of My mercy are drawn by means of one vessel only, and that is—trust. The more a soul trusts, the more it will receive. Souls that trust boundlessly are a great comfort to Me, because I pour all the treasures of My graces into them."[21]

Regarding confession Jesus told Sister Faustina, "Tell souls that from this fount of mercy souls draw graces solely with the vessel of trust. If their trust is great, there is no limit to My generosity. The torrents of grace inundate humble souls."[22]

Pray, pray much, for the virtue of trust.

The Cross

Bearing a cross for the Lord is not optional for the Christian. Jesus said, "If any man would come after me, let him deny himself and take up his cross and follow me. For whoever would save his life will lose it, and whoever loses his life for my sake will find it" (Matthew 16:24, 25).

The cross is a necessary condition to follow Christ, and paradoxically, those who are willing to lose all for Christ will gain happiness. Those who try to find happiness by avoiding suffering will never find it.

Saint Thomas Aquinas wrote, "[T]he passion of Christ completely suffices to fashion our lives. Whoever wishes to live perfectly should do nothing but disdain what Christ disdained on the cross and desire what he desired, for the cross exemplifies every virtue."[23]

Jesus emphasized the importance of the cross when Peter tried to dissuade Him from it. He told him, "Get behind me, Satan!" (Matthew 16:23). Satan is the enemy of the cross. Archbishop Fulton Sheen put it well: "When the devil is stripped of all his trappings, the ultimate goal of the demonic is to avoid the Cross, mortification, self-discipline and self-denial."[24] Jesus told Rose of Lima, "Without the cross [souls] can find no road to climb to heaven."[25]

Should we ask for suffering? An article in a Catholic magazine some years ago suggested that we should not. Alas, the author failed to consider the very prayer of the Church. For example, in the intercessions for Morning Prayer, Easter Sunday: "Lord, you walked the way of suffering and crucifixion / —may we suffer and die with you and rise again to share your glory."[26] And in the opening prayer for the Mass of Saints Philip and James (May 3), we find, "God our Father, / every year you give us joy / on the festival of the apostles Philip and James. / By the help of their prayers / may we share in the suffering, death and resurrection of your only Son / and come to the eternal vision of your glory."[27]

Lex orandi, lex credendi, "The norm of prayer is the norm of belief."

Some people are reluctant to pray for suffering, but I believe that by asking for the suffering, grace and humility to become a saint, we are likely to suffer less and more sweetly than if we did not pray for it. John Vianney said, "He who goes to meet the Cross, is in fact avoiding crosses."[28] And another John—John of the Cross—wrote, "He who seeks not the cross of Christ seeks not the glory of Christ."[29]

Pope Benedict XVI explained:

It is when we attempt to avoid suffering by withdrawing from anything that might involve hurt, when we try to spare ourselves the effort and pain of pursuing truth, love, and goodness, that we drift into a life of emptiness, in which there may be almost no pain, but the dark sensation of meaninglessness and abandonment is all the greater. It is not by sidestepping or fleeing from suffering that we are healed, but rather by our capacity for accepting it, maturing through it and finding meaning through union with Christ, who suffered with infinite love.[30]

What does it mean to "carry our cross"? It means to embrace every trial, every setback, every illness or injury, every bit of suffering we face, for love of God and for the remission of sins. It also means fasting and doing penance in accord with reason (but never *beyond* reason!).

Which is more beneficial, to choose our penances or to accept what God sends us? Although we should do both, Saint Francis de Sales "preferred chance mortifications, however small, which came unsought, to bigger things done by personal choice, and he used to say, 'Where there is less of our own choice there is more of God.'" Some of the chance mortifications he accepted willingly were "when people stopped him from getting on with some urgent business, when he met with opposition [or] came across difficult people.... And he never complained."[31]

In the Letter to the Philippians we are warned, "For many, of whom I have often told you and now tell you weeping as well, go around in a way which reveals them to be enemies of the cross of Christ. They will end in disaster! Their God is their belly; their glory is in their shame. They are set upon worldly things. But our citizenship is in heaven" (Philippians 3:18–20, author's translation).

Devotion to the Angels
It seems that the more we call on our guardian angels, the more aid we receive. After seldom praying to my angel for several years, I read the following story.

A young woman was returning to her home in Brooklyn, and as she neared her destination, she saw a menacing man leaning against a building. She prayed, "Guardian angel, protect me," and walked calmly by the man. When she was out of his sight, she ran the rest of the way home, and once inside her apartment she immediately locked the door.

The next day the young woman heard from a neighbor that a rape had occurred in the very place where she saw the man, and just after she had passed by. She offered to describe the man to the police, since she suspected he was the guilty one. They had already arrested someone and invited her down to pick him out of a lineup. She did, and then she asked one of the officers why the man hadn't gone after her.

The officer wondered about this too, so he described her to the assailant and asked why he had done nothing to her. His reply: "I remember her. But why would I have bothered her? She was walking down the street with two big guys, one on either side."[32]

This and other stories convinced me that I had paid too little attention to my angel in the past. From then on I called on him often, and I believe I've gotten more protection as a result.

A number of saints had great devotion to their guardian angel, including Saint Francis de Sales, Saint Bernard, Saint Rose of Lima and Saint Jerome. God has given us each a heavenly protector. We should make use of that gift daily.

Persevere

Perseverance may not qualify as a short way to the kingdom, but it is a sure way nonethless. Resolve never to give up praying and striving for virtue, no matter how many times you fall.

Jesus promised us success: "I tell you, Ask, and it will be given you; seek, and you will find; knock, and it will be opened to you. For every one who asks receives, and he who seeks finds, and to him who knocks it will be opened" (Luke 11:9–10).

In this book I have presented many tried-and-true means of becoming holy. But you can't start all these things at once. You should work at one or two things at a time. Remember, becoming holy is a lifelong project. Yes, your life: that's exactly how much time you have to prepare for your great homecoming, that day when the Lord will say to you, "Well done, good and faithful servant."

This process of holiness is primarily the Lord's work in you. Allow Him to guide you in your journey toward heaven. He will show you what is right for your spiritual life at the various stages of your life. How do you get that guidance? By growing slowly but surely in prayer and by reading the lives of the saints. As the saints knew well, holiness is the shortest way to the kingdom, and the happiest way to live.

> May the God of peace himself make you completely holy
> and may you be kept entirely blameless
> —spirit, soul, and body—
> or the coming of our Lord Jesus Christ.
> The one who calls you is faithful,
> and he will do it. (1 Thessalonians 5:23–24, author's translation)

. . . . .

AFTERWORD

Thank you for reading this book. I sincerely hope it will help you draw closer to God and to His kingdom. If you would like to tell me how this book has helped—or not—kindly e-mail me at frmorrow@ mindspring.com.

. . . . .

. . . . .

NOTES

PART ONE: MOTIVATIONS FOR HOLINESS
Chapter One: The Delight of Heaven: The Divine Marriage

1. John K. Ryan, trans., *The Confessions of St. Augustine* (New York: Image, 1960), bk. 10, chap. 27, pp. 254–255.
2. Council of Florence, Session 6, July 6, 1439, available at: www.ewtn.com.
3. Teresa of Avila, *The Way of Perfection*, E. Allison Peers, trans. (New York: Image, 1964), chap. 2, no. 7, p. 43.
4. John of the Cross, *The Spiritual Canticle*, in Kieran Kavanaugh and Otilio Rodriguez, trans., *The Collected Works of St. John of the Cross* (Washington, D.C.: ICS, 1979), p. 450.
5. Gregory the Great, Sermon of the Second Sunday After Pentecost, no. 9, M.F. Toal, ed., *The Sunday Sermons of the Great Fathers* (San Francisco: Ignatius, 2000), vol. 3, p. 186.
6. John of the Cross, *The Spiritual Canticle*, in *Collected Works*, p. 497.
7. Teresa of Avila, *Spiritual Testimonies*, in Kieran Kavanaugh and Otilio Rodriguez, trans., *The Collected Works of St. Teresa of Ávila*, vol. 1 (Washington, D.C.: ICS, 1976), p. 336.
8. See Francis Trochu, *The Curé d'Ars: St. Jean-Marie Baptiste Vianney*, Dom Ernest Graf, trans. (Rockford, Ill.: TAN, 1977), p. 545.
9. Sisters of the Visitation, trans., *Autobiography of St. Margaret Mary Alacoque* (Rockford, Ill.: TaN, 1986), p. 40.
10. *Autobiography of St. Margaret Mary Alacoque*, p. 64.
11. John of the Cross, *The Spiritual Canticle*, in *Collected Works*, pp. 474–475.
12. This takes more imagination for men than for women, to be sure. However, the *Catechism of the Catholic Church* teaches, "We ought therefore to recall that God transcends the human distinction between the sexes. He is neither man nor woman: he is God" (CCC, #239). We call Him by male names and pronouns because He has a male role in relationship to us (provider, pursuer and so on). Thus the soul is always feminine in spiritual writing. Men who have difficulty imagining this embrace should realize that both men and women are created in the image and likeness of God. When a man sees the beauty of a woman, body and soul, he sees a reflection of the beauty of God.

It should be realized that such a fantasy focused on God could be taken to immoral extremes. However, if your thoughts become sexual, you should simply fast-forward through that to a more sedate sharing of affection.

13. Pope Benedict XVI, *Deus Caritas Est*, 2005, no. 9, available at: www. ewtn.com.

Chapter Two: The Reality of Hell

1. Josemaría Escrivá, *The Way* (Manila: Scriptor, 1982), no. 749, p. 206.

2. Catherine of Siena, "A Treatise of Discretion," in Algar Thorold, trans., *The Dialogue of St. Catherine of Siena* (Rockford, Ill.: Tan, 1974), p. 105.

3. Augustine, *The City of God*, chap. 23, no. 23, as quoted in John Hardon, "Demons are the Angels Who Fell by Their Discobedience to the Will of God," available at: www.therealpresence.org.

4. Saint Francis de Sales, *Introduction to The Devout Life* (London: Rivingtons, 1876), pp. 41, 42, available at: www.ccel.org.

5. See Ignatius of Loyola, *Spiritual Exercises*, Elder Mullan, trans., 1909, First Week, Fifth Exercise, available at: www.ewtn.com.

6. John Chrysostom, Homily 15, in *St. Chrysostom: On the Priesthood; Ascetic Treatises; Select Homilies and Letters; Homilies on the Statutes*, in Philip Schaff, *Nicene and Post-Nicene Fathers*, available at: www.ccel.org.

7. Teresa of Avila, *The Book of Her Life*, in *Collected Works*, vol. 1, p. 213.

Chapter Three: The Suffering of Purgatory

1. Adapted from the *RSV* Bible, Catholic Edition. Some other biblical passages that support the teaching on purgatory: "And in anger his lord delivered him to the jailers, till he should pay all his debt. So also my heavenly Father will do to every one of you, if you do not forgive your brother from your heart" (Matthew 18:34–35). The implication here is that one may make up for sins after death. Also we read, "Therefore [Judas Maccabeus] made atonement for the dead, that they might be delivered from their sin" (2 Maccabees 12:45). Prayer for the dead is linked to the doctrine of purgatory, since if the dead are in heaven or hell, there is no need or no reason to pray for them. See also Matthew 12:32.

2. Council of Trent, Session 25, December 3, 4, 1563: Decree Concerning Purgatory, in *The Canons and Decrees of the Council of Trent*, H.J. Schroeder, trans. (Rockford, Ill.: Tan, 1978), p. 214.

3. Serge Hughes, trans., *Catherine of Genoa: Purgation and Purgatory* (Mahwah, N.J.: Paulist, 1979), p. 78.

4. C.S. Lewis, *Letters to Malcolm: Chiefly on Prayer* (Orlando: Harvest, 2002), pp. 108–109.

5. Quoted in Thomas Aquinas, *Summa Theologica*, Supplement, app. 1, ques. 2, art. 1, Fathers of the English Dominican Province, trans. (New York: Benziger, 1948), vol. 3, p. 3018.

6. Thomas Aquinas, *Summa*, app. 1, ques. 2, art. 1, p. 3018.

7. Francis de Sales, in *Esprit de Francis de Sales*, chap. 9, p. 16, as quoted in F.X. Schouppe, *Purgatory: Illustrated by the Lives and Legends of the Saints* (Rockford, Ill.: Tan, 1986), p. 27.

8. Anthony Mottola, trans., *The Spiritual Exercises of St. Ignatius* (Garden City, N.Y.: Image, 1964), 2nd week, 12th day, p. 82.

9. Catherine of Genoa, *The Life and Doctrine of Saint Catherine of Genoa*, Christian Press Association, New York, trans., chap. 22, available at: www.ccel.org.

10. Pope John Paul II, General Audience, August 4, 1999, "Purgatory Is Necessary Purification," no. 5, available at: www.ewtn.com.

11. Teresa of Avila, *Way of Perfection*, chap. 40, p. 266.

12. Pope Paul VI, *Apostolic Constitution on the Revision of Indulgences*, 2, as quoted in United States Conference of Catholic Bishops, *Manual of Indulgences: Norms and Grants* (Washington, D.C.: USCCB, 2006), p. 122.

13. Catherine of Genoa, as quoted in Schouppe, p. 287.

14. Robert Bellarmine, *De Gemitu*, bk. 2, chap. 9, as quoted in Schouppe, p. 68.

15. Reginald Garrigou-Lagrange, *Life Everlasting and the Immensity of the Soul: A Theological Treatise on the Four Last Things: Death, Judgment, Heaven, Hell* (Rockford, Ill.: Tan, 1991), p. 177.

16. James Alberione, *Lest We Forget* (Boston: Daughters of St. Paul, 1967), p. 77.

17. *Life and Doctrine of Saint Catherine of Genoa* (New York: Christian Press Association, 1907), Spiritual Dialogue Part First, chap. 16, available at: www.ccel.org.

18. Garrigou-Lagrange, p. 177.

19. *Summa*, ques. 10, art. 5, vol. 1, p. 43.

20. Teresa of Avila, *Foundations*, chap. 10, in *Collected Works*, vol. 3, pp. 145–146; Marcelle Auclair, *Saint Teresa of Ávila* (New York: Pantheon, 1953), pp. 188–189.

21. Peter Lappin, *Give Me Souls!: Life of Don Bosco* (New Rochelle, N.Y.: Don Bosco, 1986), p. 188.

22. *Autobiography of St. Margaret Mary Alacoque*, pp. 110–111.

23. Teresa of Avila, *The Book of Her Life*, chap. 38, no. 29, in *Collected Works*, vol. 1, p. 266.

24. Teresa of Avila, *The Book of Her Life*, chap. 38, no. 31, pp. 266–267.

25. Teresa of Avila, *The Book of Her Life*, chap. 38, no. 32, p. 267.

Chapter Four: The Pursuit of Happiness

1. From *Liturgy of the Hours*, vol. 1 (New York: Catholic Book, 1975), p. 1067.

2. Pope John Paul II, *Redemptor Hominis*, 10, available at: www.ewtn.com.

3. Pope Benedict XVI, *Deus Caritas Est*, 6, available at: www.ewtn.com.
4. Pope Benedict XVI, Apostolic Exhortation *Sacramentum Caritatis*, 3, 17, 70, 77, 84, 93, available at: www.ewtn.com.

PART TWO: THE LIFE OF GRACE
Chapter Five: The Foundation: Prayer
1. May 13 was the date of the first apparition of Mary at Fatima. It was at one of the subsequent apparitions there that Mary predicted the Russian takeover of many countries.
2. See Albert Shamon, *The Power of the Rosary* (Oak Lawn, Ill.: CMJ Marian, 1990), pp. 30–31.
3. John Beevers, trans., *The Autobiography of St. Thérèse of Lisieux: The Story of a Soul* (Garden City, N.Y.: Image, 1957), p. 136.
4. "The Blessing of Unanswered Prayer," available at: www.godweb.org.
5. Beevers, p. 109.

Chapter Six: Beginning Prayer
1. See www.radicalforgiveness.com and Fred Luskin, *Forgive for Good* (San Francisco: HarperCollins, 2002), pp. 78–79.
2. Teresa of Avila, *Way of Perfection*, chap. 25, no. 1, in *Collected Works*, vol. 2, p. 131.
3. Sophia Michalenko, *Mercy My Mission: Life of Sister Faustina H. Kowalska* (Stockbridge, Mass.: Marian, 1987), p. 215.
4. Faustina Kowalska, *Divine Mercy in My Soul: The Diary of the Servant of God Sister M. Faustina Kowalska* (Stockbridge, Mass.: Marian, 1990), no. 1076, p. 404.
5. Trochu, p. 310.
6. Francis de Sales, *Introduction to the Devout Life*, John K. Ryan, trans. (New York: Image, 1955), p. 105.

Chapter Seven: Spiritual Reading
1. Saint Jerome, as cited in Alphonsus Ligouri "On Spiritual Reading," available at: www.ourladyswarriors.org.
2. Francis de Sales, *Introduction to the Devout Life*, p. 108.
3. Francis de Sales, quoted in Tony Jones, *The Sacred Way: Spiritual Practices for Everyday Life* (Grand Rapids, Mich.: Zondervan, 2005), p. 54.
4. To see a list of recommended spiritual reading that I have compiled, go to www. cfalive.org.
5. John Clarke, O.C.D., trans., *St. Thérèse of Lisieux: Her Last Conversations* (Washington, D.C.: ICS, 1977), p. 5.
6. Athanasius, as quoted in Ronda Chervin, *Quotable Saints* (Ann Arbor, Mich.: Servant, 1992), p. 138.

Chapter Eight: Meditation and Contemplation

1. This is based in part on Sam Anthony Morello, Lectio Divina *and the Practice of Teresian Prayer* (Washington, D.C.: ICS, 1995), pp. 20–25; and Thomas Dubay, *Prayer Primer: Igniting a Fire Within* (Cincinnati: Servant, 2002), pp. 70–71.
2. To see a booklet by the author on the Stations of the Cross go to www.cfalive.org.
3. Faustina Kowalska, *Divine Mercy in My Soul*, p. 166.
4. Two such booklets on the rosary by the author can be found at www.cfalive.org.
5. Louis de Montfort, *Methods for Saying the Rosary*, in *God Alone: The Collected Writings of St. Louis Marie de Montfort* (Bayshore, N.Y.: Montfort, 1987), p. 237. For the papal recommendations, see Pope John Paul II's *Rosarium virginis Mariae*, no. 33 and Paul VI's *Marialis Cultis*, no. 46, available at: www.vatican.va.
6. "Protestants and the Rosary," available at: www.rosaryworkshop.com.
7. Pope John Paul II, *Familiaris Consortio*, 61, www.ewtn.com. This is a quote from Pope Paul VI, *Marialis Cultus*, 52, 54.
8. Pope John Paul II and Pope Benedict XV, quoted at www.mgr.org.
9. William Thomas Walsh, *Our Lady of Fátima* (New York: Image, 1954), pp. 52, 80, 81.
10. Thomas Dubay, *Fire Within: St. Teresa of Avila, St. John of the Cross, and the Gospel—on Prayer* (San Francisco: Ignatius, 1989), p. 57.
11. Teresa of Avila, *Book of Her Life*, chap. 39, section 23, p. 275.
12. Teresa of Avila, *Book of Her Life*, chap. 22, sec. 10, p. 148.
13. Dubay, *Fire Within*, p. 59.
14. Dubay, *Fire Within*, p. 60.

Chapter Nine: Difficulties in Prayer

1. Teresa of Avila, *Book of Her Life*, chap. 8, sec. 7, p. 68.
2. Teresa of Avila, *Book of Her Life*, chap. 19, sec. 4, p. 124.
3. Teresa of Avila, available at: www.sacredheartmanassas.org.
4. Thérèse of Lisieux, available at: http://infomotions.com.
5. See two by this author at www.cfalive.org.
6. There are several recordings of the rosary available. Search the Internet for "rosary recordings."
7. Teresa of Avila, *Spiritual Testimonies*, no. 39, in *Collected Works*, vol. 1, p. 341.
8. Teresa of Avila, *Interior Castle*, in *Collected Works*, vol. 2, p. 450.
9. Francis de Sales, as quoted in R.P. Quadrupani, *Light and Peace: Instructions for Devout Souls to Dispel Their Doubts and Allay Their Fears* (Rockford, Ill.: Tan, 1980), p. 51.
10. Francis de Sales, as quoted in Quadrupani, p. 23.

Chapter Ten: Commitment to Prayer

1. Teresa of Avila, as quoted at www.opnunslancaster.org.
2. John Vianney, as quoted in Jill Haak Adels, *The Wisdom of the Saints: An Anthology* (Oxford: Oxford University Press, 1987), p. 40.
3. Alphonsus Liguori, *To Serve Christ Jesus* (Monroe, Mich.: Sisters, Servants of the Immaculate Heart of Mary, 1974), p. 51.
4. John of the Cross, as quoted in Suzanne Clores, *The Wisdom of the Saints* (New York: Citadel, 2002), p. 115.

Chapter Eleven: The Sacrament of Penance

1. Pope John Paul II, *Reconciliatio et Paenitentia* (On Reconciliation and Penance), 32, available at: www.ewtn.com.
2. Pius XII, *Mystici Corporis Christi*, (on the Mystical Body of Christ), 88, available at: www.vatican.va.
3. Francis de Sales, *Introduction to the Devout Life*, pp. 11–12.
4. George William Rutler, *Saint John Vianney, The Curé d'Ars Today* (San Francisco: Ignatius, 1988), p. 153.
5. Abbot Dorotheus, as quoted at www.lifeofprayer.org.

Chapter Twelve: The Mass, "Source and Summit of the Christian Life"

1. Pope John Paul II, *Dominicae Cenae* (On the Mystery and Worship of the Eucharist), 9, available at: www.ewtn.com.
2. Council of Trent, Session 22, Doctrine Concerning the Sacrifice of the Mass, September 17, 1562, chap. 1, available at: www.ewtn.com.
3. Council of Trent, Session 13, October 11, 1551, canon 1, available at: www.ewtn.com.
4. Joan Carroll Cruz, *Eucharistic Miracles and Eucharistic Phenomena in the Lives of the Saints* (Rockford, Ill.: Tan, 1987), p. 3.
5. Cruz, pp. 3–7.
6. Vatican II, *Sacrosanctum Concilium* (Constitution on the Sacred Liturgy), 10, available at: www.ewtn.com.
7. Bernard of Clairvaux, as quoted in Stefano Manelli, *Jesus Our Eucharistic Love: Eucharistic Life According to the examples of the Saints* (Manila: Immaculata Formation House, 1973), p. 22.
8. Francis de Sales, *Introduction to the Devout Life*, chap. 14, nos. 1, 2, p. 98, available at: www.ccel.org.
9. Council of Trent, Session 25, available at: www.ewtn.com.
10. John Vianney, as quoted in Manelli, p. 33.
11. Pope John Paul II, *Dies Domini* (on Keeping the Lord's Day Holy), 61, available at: www.ewtn.com.
12. Francis de Sales, *Introduction to the Devout Life*, chap. 14, no. 3, pp. 98, 99, available at: www.ccel.org.

Chapter Thirteen: Eucharistic Adoration
1. The story of Bishop Sheen and the Chinese girl is from www.tldm.org.
2. Adapted from Trochu, p. 184.

PART THREE: LOVING OUR NEIGHBOR
Chapter Fourteen: The Spiritual Works of Mercy
1. *Summa*, II IIae, ques. 32, art. 3, vol. 2, p. 1326.
2. Pope Paul VI, *Evangelii Nuntiandi*, 24, available at: www.ewtn.com.
3. Pope John Paul II, *Redemptoris Missio* (On the Permanent Validity of the Church's Missionary Mandate), 11, available at: www.ewtn.com. In no. 72 John Paul gives examples of how the laity can evangelize.
4. Carlo Carretto, *Letters from the Desert* in *Carlo Carretto: Selected Writings* (Maryknoll, N.Y.: Orbis, 1972), p. 32, available at: www.maryknoll-mall.org.
5. Walsh, p. 120.
6. John Clarke, O.C.D., trans., *Story of a Soul: The Autobiography of St. Thérèse of Lisieux*, (Washington, D.C.: ICS, 1999), pp. 99–100.
7. Ambrose, as quoted in Alberione, pp. 106–107.
8. Cited in Alberione, pp. 111–112.
9. Alberione, p. 125.
10. Council of Trent, session 25, available at: www.ewtn.com.
11. There are others associated with churches or certain days. For a list of works for plenary and partial indulgences, see www.catholic.org.
12. The traditional period of eight days was expanded to twenty days in the Decree of the Apostolic Penitentiary in the Jubilee Year 2000, *The Gift of the Indulgence* (no. 5). In February of 2005 the Apostolic Penitentiary confirmed, in response to a question raised by EWTN, that this norm remains in effect and was not limited to the jubilee year (see www.ewtn.com).
13. See Apostolic Penitentiary, *Manual of Indulgences: Norms and Grants* (Washington, D.C.: USCCB, 2006), pp. 18, 41.
14. Alberione, p. 151.
15. Alberione, p. 164.
16. *Manual of Indulgences*, p. 7.
17. John Bosco, *The Life of St. Dominic Savio*, Paul Aronica, trans., (Paterson, N.J.: Salesiana, 1955), p. 16; and Peter Lappin, *Dominic Savio: Teenage Saint* (New Rochelle, N.Y.: Salesiana, 1965), pp. 48–49.

Chapter Fifteen: The Corporal Works of Mercy
1. Pope John Paul II, homily at Yankee Stadium, October 2, 1979, available at: www.emmitsburg.net.

2. Ignatius of Loyola, Prayer for Generosity, available at: http://www.bc.edu.

3. Pope John Paul II, "Letter to Families," February 1994, no.22, available at: www.ewtn.com.

4. Pope John Paul II, *Centesimus Annus*, no. 42, available at: www.ewtn.com.

5. The Pontifical Council for the pastoral care of migrants and itinerant people, Instruction *Erga migrantes caritas Christi* (The Love of Christ toward Migrants), 2004, nos. 39, 40. This document and referenced documents are all avalable at: www.ewtn.com.

6. Igino Giordani, *St. Catherine of Siena—Doctor of the Church*, Thomas J. Tobin, trans., (Boston: Daughters of St. Paul, 1975), pp. 63–64, and Raymond of Capua, *The Life of Catherine of Siena*, Conleth Kearns, trans., (Washington, D.C.: Dominicana, 1994), pp. 152–153.

7. Based on a story found at www.encyclopedia.com.

8. William R. Bonniwell, *The Life of Blessed Margaret of Castello, 1287–1320* (Madison, Wisc.: Idea, 1979), p. 83.

9. Bonniwell, pp. 95–96.

PART FOUR: THE LIFE OF VIRTUE

Chapter Sixteen: The Theological Virtues: Faith, Hope and Charity

1. Teresa of Avila, *The Interior Castle*, VII: 4, no. 9, in *Collected Works*, vol. 1, p. 44.

2. Augustine, according to *Summa*, II IIae, ques. 2, art.1, p. 1179.

3. Augustine, Tractate 29 on the Gospel of John, no. 6, available at: www.newadvent.org.

4. *Code of Canon Law*, Canon 750, available at: www.vatican.va.

5. Vatican II, *Lumen Gentium*, Dogmatic Constitution on the Church, no. 25, available at: www.ewtn.com.

6. John Henry Newman, as quoted in *The Liturgy of the Hours*, vol. 4 (New York: Catholic Book, 1975), p. 628.

7. Josef Pieper, *Faith, Hope, Love*, Richard and Clara Winston and Mary F. McCarthy, trans., (San Francisco: Ignatius, 1997), p. 98.

8. J. Neuner and J. Dupuis, *The Christian Faith in the Doctrinal Documents of the Catholic Church* (New York: Alba, 1996), no. 1976, p. 764.

9. Pope Benedict XVI, *Spe Salvi*, nos. 26, 32, available at: www.ewtn.com.

10. Pieper, *Faith, Hope, Love*, p. 110. Thomas Aquinas quote is from *Summa*, I IIae, ques. 40, art. 6.

11. Neuner and Dupuis, no. 1942, p. 757.

12. Augustine, *Sermons*, 87, 8, as quoted in Pieper, p. 113.

13. Pieper, p. 113.

14. Faustina Kowalska, *Divine Mercy in My Soul*, no. 1059, pp. 399, 400.

15. *Dialogue of Saint Catherine of Siena*, p. 267.
16. Mother Teresa, as quoted at www.ascension-research.org.
17. *Dialogue of St. Catherine of Siena*, p. 196.

Chapter Seventeen: Prudence, Justice and Fortitude
1. Quoted in Joseph Pieper, *The Four Cardinal Virtues: Prudence, Justice, Fortitude, Temperance* (Notre Dame, Ind.: University of Notre Dame Press, 1966), p. 64.
2. *Eucharistiae Sacramentum*, no. 84: "Genuflection in the presence of the Blessed Sacrament, whether reserved in the tabernacle or exposed for public adoration, is on one knee." www.ewtn.com.
3. Gregory the Great, as quoted in *Summa*, II IIae, ques. 104, art. 3, vol. 2, p. 1643.
4. William Thomas Walsh, *Saint Teresa of Ávila: A Biography* (Milwaukee: Bruce, 1943), pp. 446–447.
5. Philip Neri, as quoted in Quadrupani, p. 1.
6. Michalenko, p. 137.
7. Regarding the speed limit, most safe-driving advocates suggest staying within five miles per hour over the speed limit. It seems this is because officials keep the limits unduly low, knowing that drivers will exceed them by a certain amount no matter where they are set.
8. *Summa*, II IIae, ques. 110, art. 3, Reply Obj. 4 , vol. 2, p. 1667.
9. Pieper, *The Four Cardinal Virtues*, p. 117.
10. *Summa*, II IIae, ques. 123, art. 5, vol. 2, p. 1710.
11. From Enzo Lodi, *Saints of the Roman Calendar*, Jordan Aumann, trans., (New York: Alba, 1992), p. 67.

Chapter Eighteen: Temperance
1. Karol Wojtyla, *Love and Responsibility*, H.T. Willetts, trans., (New York: Farrar, Straus, Giroux, 1981), p. 198.
2. Jerome, as quoted in *Summa*, II IIae, ques. 147, art. 1, vol. 2, p. 1785.
3. Augustine, Sermon 73, On Prayer and Fasting, as quoted in *Summa*, II IIae, ques. 147, art. 1, vol. 2, p. 1785.
4. *Summa*, ques. 147, art. 3, available at: www.newadvent.org.
5. *Code of Canon Law*, no. 1249, available at: www.vatican.va.
6. *Dialogue of St. Catherine of Siena*, p. 55.
7. *Treasure in Clay: The Autobiography of Fulton J. Sheen* (New York: Doubleday, 1980), p. 268.
8. See author's article on modesty at www.cfalive.org.
9. Thomas Dubay, *Happy Are You Poor: The Simple Life and Spiritual Freedom*, 2nd ed. (San Francisco: Ignatius, 2003), p. 13.
10. Ignatius of Loyola, *Spiritual Exercises* (Garden City, N.Y.: Image, 1964), p. 76.

11. Ambrose, *De Nabuthe*, c. 12, n. 53 (P.L. 14, 747), as quoted in Pope Paul VI, *Populorum Progressio*, Encyclical on the Development of Peoples, March 26, 1967, no. 23, www.ewtn.com.

12. *Familiaris Consortio*, no. 37, available at: www.newadvent.org.

Chapter Nineteen: The Fruits of the Holy Spirit

1. Beevers, pp. 126–127; Clarke, pp. 222–223.

2. Father Cuthbert, *The Life of St. Francis of Assisi* (London: Longmans Green, 1921), p. 180.

3. Some of these points are drawn from Mary Mercedes, *A Book of Courtesy*, revised by her students (San Francisco: Harper, 2001). Others the author added.

4. Thomas Aquinas, *Summa*, II IIae, ques. 158, art. 1, vol. 2, p. 1838.

5. Bonaventure, as quoted in Alban Butler, *The Lives of the Fathers, Martyrs, and Other Principal Saints* (Dublin: J. Duffy, 1866), p. 146.

6. Omer Englebert, *Saint Francis of Assisi: A Biography*, Eve Marie Cooper, trans., (Ann Arbor, Mich.: Servant, 1979), p. 84.

7. John Henry Newman, *Parochial Sermons* (New York: Appleton, 1843), vol. 1, p. 194.

8. Clare of Assisi, as quoted in Adels, p. 193.

9. John of Vianney, as quoted in Adels, p. 193.

10. Merlin R. Carothers, *Power in Praise* (Escondido, Calif.: Carothers, 1972), p. 104.

11. John Henry Newman, Sermon 19, "The Blessings of This Life," *Parochial Sermons* (London: Rivington, 1840), vol. 5, p. 307.

12. Thomas Aquinas, as quoted in Adels, p. 191.

13. The Serenity Prayer as we have quoted it is different from the popularized one but appears to be the original. Available at: http://skdesigns.com.

14. Augustine, *Confessions*, bk. 1, chap. 1, no. 1, p. 43.

Chapter Twenty: The Shortest Way to the Kingdom

1. *Manual of Indulgences*, USCCB translation, pp. 25–36.

2. For a list of works for plenary and partial indulgences, see www.catholic.org.

3. Pope Pius XII, *Mediator Dei* (On the Sacred Liturgy), 176, available at: www.ewtn.com.

4. Adapted from Trochu, p. 540.

5. Louis de Montfort, "True Devotion to Mary," no. 115, in *God Alone: The Collected Writings of St. Louis Marie de Montfort* (Bay Shore, N.Y.: Montfort, 1995), pp. 324–325.

6. Fulton J. Sheen, *The World's First Love* (New York: McGraw-Hill, 1952), pp. 188, 189.

7. Available at: www.memorare.com.

8. Augustine, Letter 118, 22, as quoted at www.opusdei.us.

9. Michael de la Bedoyere, *Francois de Sales* (in print today under the title *The Saint Maker*, Sophia Press) (New York: Harper, 1960), p. 245.

10. Rafael Cardinal Merry del Val (1865–1930), Secretary of State for Pope Saint Pius X, "Litany of Humility." A slightly different version is available at: www.ewtn.com.

11. Alphonsus Rodriguez, quoted at http://newsgroups.derkeiler.com.

12. Marcelle Auclair, *Saint Teresa of Ávila* (New York: Pantheon, 1953), p. 363.

13. *Autobiography of St. Margaret Mary Alacoque*, no. 47, pp. 61–62.

14. Michalenko, pp. 31, 32.

15. Adapted from www.ewtn.com.

16. Michalenko, pp. 120, 127. This differs from a plenary indulgence in that it is given directly by Christ, not through the Church.

17. Michalenko, p. 113.

18. See Colin B. Donovan, "Mercy Sunday or Feast of Mercy," available at: www.ewtn.com.

19. Faustina Kowalska, *Divine Mercy in My Soul*, no. 742, pp. 297–298.

20. Michalenko, p. 152.

21. Michalenko, p. 215.

22. Michalenko, p. 218.

23. Thomas Aquinas, from a conference, in *The Liturgy of the Hours*, vol. 3 (New York: Catholic Book, 1975), p. 22.

24. Sheen, *Treasure in Clay*, p. 334.

25. Rose of Lima, quoted in Marcellino d'Ambrosio, "The Beauty of Divine Grace," available at: www.crossroadsinitiative.com.

26. Easter Sunday Morning Prayer, *The Liturgy of the Hours According to the Roman Rite* (New York: Catholic Book, 1976), vol. 2, p. 525.

27. There are other examples, such as the closing prayer for the Mass of the Holy Rosary (October 7), closing prayer for Evening Prayer, Friday, week 3, and final intercession for Morning Prayer, second Wednesday of Lent.

28. Alfred Monnin, *The Curé of Ars*, Bertram Wolferstam, trans., (St. Louis: Herder, 1924), p. 165.

29. From *Collected Works of St. John of the Cross*, no. 102, available at: www.karmel.at.

30. Pope Benedict XVI, *Spe Salvi*, no. 37, available at: www.ewtn.com.

31. Elisabeth Stopp, trans., *St. Francis de Sales: A Testimony by St. Chantal* (London: Faber and Faber, 1967), p. 81.

32. Joan Wester Anderson, *Where Angels Walk* (New York: Ballantine, 1993), pp. 93–95.

. . . . .